Knowing Him by Name

Knowing Him by Name

Short Devotional Readings on the Names and References to God the Father, God the Son, and God the Holy Spirit

LEWIS G. LARKING

RESOURCE *Publications* · Eugene, Oregon

KNOWING HIM BY NAME
Short Devotional Readings on the Names and References to God the Father, God the Son, and God the Holy Spirit

Copyright © 2019 Lewis G. Larking. All rights reserved. Except for brief quotations in critical publications or reviews, no part of this book may be reproduced in any manner without prior written permission from the publisher. Write: Permissions, Wipf and Stock Publishers, 199 W. 8th Ave., Suite 3, Eugene, OR 97401.

Resource Publications
An Imprint of Wipf and Stock Publishers
199 W. 8th Ave., Suite 3
Eugene, OR 97401

www.wipfandstock.com

PAPERBACK ISBN: 978-1-5326-7382-5
HARDCOVER ISBN: 978-1-5326-7383-2
EBOOK ISBN: 978-1-5326-7384-9

Manufactured in the U.S.A.   FEBRUARY 1, 2019

All Scripture quotations, unless otherwise indicated, are taken from the Holy Bible, New International Version®, NIV®. Copyright ©1973, 1978, 1984, 2011 by Biblica, Inc.™ Used by permission of Zondervan. All rights reserved worldwide. www.zondervan.com The "NIV" and "New International Version" are trademarks registered in the United States Patent and Trademark Office by Biblica, Inc.™

Scriptures marked KJV are taken from the KING JAMES VERSION (KJV): KING JAMES VERSION, public domain.

Scripture quotations marked RSV are taken from the Revised Standard Version of the Bible, copyright © 1946, 1952, and 1971 National Council of the Churches of Christ in the United States of America. Used by permission. All rights reserved worldwide.

Contents

Preface | vii

Introduction | ix

Abbreviations | x

Names for, and References to, God the Father | 1

Names for, and References to, God the Son, our Lord Jesus Christ | 69

Names for, and References to, God the Holy Spirit | 147

Index of Names for, and References to, God the Father | 177

Index of Names for, and References to, God the Son | 179

Index of Names for, and References to, God the Holy Spirit | 181

Preface

"Knowing Him by Name" is a series of short devotional studies on the names and references to God the Father, God the Son, and God the Holy Spirit. Each reading was limited to around 175 words and prepared for the weekly Church Bulletin at the Mueller Community Church, Rothwell, Queensland, Australia.

This collection is now dedicated to my dearest wife June and our children Christopher and Margaret, and their respective families. I also thank June and Margaret for their typing and editing of the text.

The readings come to you, and to the wider Christian community, with my prayer that in reading about these names and references to God you will want to know him better. As God said to Jeremiah: *"let him who boasts boast about this: that he understands and knows me,"* (9:24). I trust you will want to make this your boast.

Introduction

A NAME REPRESENTS THE person who owns the name. When we read the many names, titles and metaphors referring to God the Father, the Lord Jesus Christ and the Holy Spirit, they reveal something about God's character. Therefore to understand a name is to know something of God's nature and person.

Increasing our understanding of God so that we can "know him" must be a priority for every Christian. It was the Apostle Paul's ambition: *I want to know Christ and the power of his resurrection,* (Philippians 3:10).

As we meditate on the names of God, we can expect the Holy Spirit will use our knowledge about God to transform us into the likeness of God, (2 Corinthians 3:18).

Getting to know God will be a lifelong task. Think of it as a journey with each name of God as a road sign. Each time you read about one of his names it will point the way to him. Pray that God will help you to "know him".

Abbreviations

KJV   King James Version
NIV   New International Version
RSV   Revised Standard Version

Names for, and References to, God the Father

GOD (ELOHIM) CREATOR OF HEAVEN AND EARTH
(Genesis 14:19)

Elohim is the plural form of the Hebrew name for God that occurs about 2,500 times in the Old Testament and thirty times in the first chapter of Genesis. The name embraces the idea of his eternal being and his almighty power as the Creator.

Nine times in Genesis 1 we read that *God said*, and on each occasion something further was created. The Genesis account confirms that God saw his original creation as *very good and pleasing to him* (1:31).

Hebrews 11:3 reminds us that *what is seen was not made out of what was visible*, while Romans 4:17 states that he is the God *who gives life to the dead and calls things that are not as though they were*.

Reflection: *Being made in the image of God, and being made new in Christ Jesus means that the creative nature of God is part of our new nature. Developing our creativity should be part of our development as we grow in Christ.*

THE GREAT GOD—EL

The LORD your God (Elohim) is God of gods and Lord of lords, the great God (El), mighty and awesome, who shows no partiality and accepts no bribes, (Deuteronomy 10:17).

The shortened form of the Hebrew name "Elohim" is "El", which also has the meaning of an all-powerful God. What is significant about this title, *the Great God*, is that God revealed his greatness to Israel at a time of great need. He therefore expected them to act in ways that were upright, bringing Him honor among the nations.

As we worship the *Great God* through Christ Jesus, we also have an obligation to bring honor to Him and share his love in practical ways with others.

Reflection: *Living selfishly comes from yielding to the false gods of our culture that lead us to think we can bring security and protection to our lives through our possessions. Have you thought that when you deal uprightly with people and help the needy, you are honoring "the Great God"?*

THE LORD GOD

The LORD God formed the man from the dust of the ground, (Genesis 2:7).

In Genesis 2, the name the *LORD God* is mentioned eleven times. This is the first time the name LORD, or "YHWH" is mentioned in the Bible. Its use lets the reader know that the name "God", in the first chapter, is the same divine person that is mentioned here.

The name *LORD God* therefore combines the identity of the all-powerful Creator God with his identity as LORD, the one who is eternally self-existent and in covenant relationship with mankind. The name informs us that God intended Adam and Eve to have a special relationship with him.

However, this covenant relationship with the *LORD God* was broken through their sin of disobedience, and so they were expelled from the Garden of Eden.

Reflection: *Satan continues to deceive people into thinking they can disobey the "LORD God" and live independently of him. Rather, knowing the "LORD God" means a living relationship in dependence on him.*

GOD MOST HIGH—EL ELYON
LORD GOD MOST HIGH

Blessed be God Most High, who delivered your enemies into your hand, (Genesis 14:20).

The name *God Most High* refers to God as preeminent and supreme over all. The name occurs on the occasion when Abraham returned from a victory over the kings and was met by Melchizedek, the king of Salem and priest of *God Most High* (Genesis 14).

Melchizedek blessed him in the name of *God Most High, the Creator of heaven and earth*. Abraham was then told that God had given him his victory (14:20) and so he gave Melchizedek a tithe, or one-tenth of the spoils of the battle.

Abraham now knew who was responsible for the victory, and so he acknowledged God as the *LORD God Most High*, (14:22).

Reflection: *"The LORD God Most High" is still preeminent and ready to listen to and work on behalf of his people. Like Abraham, we too need to be generous in giving to God as an expression of our thanks.*

THE SOVEREIGN LORD—ADONAI
(Genesis 15:2)

The name "Lord", written in the Old Testament in lower case letters, refers to the majesty and authority of the Lord as Sovereign. It complements God's personal name of LORD (YHWH).

The first mention of the name was the occasion when Abraham expected a son based on God's promise (Genesis 12:2–3). Twenty years had passed and at eighty-five years of age there was still no child. Abraham shared his concern with the LORD recognizing him as Sovereign Lord (15:2). The LORD then assured him that his descendants would be as numerous as the stars of the sky.

Abraham was given new hope, but now had to continue living by faith even when he still did not see the solution to his problem.

Reflection: *Trusting God against seemingly impossible odds was not easy for Abraham and it will not be easy for us. Knowing the Lord as Sovereign and learning to believe his word and obey him is the pathway to knowing God and realizing his purposes for our lives.*

THE GOD WHO SEES ME—EL ROI
(Genesis 16:13)

Hagar had been Sarah's maid but the maid/mistress relationship changed when Sarah knew that Hagar was soon to be the mother of Abraham's child. Sarah began to mistreat her and so Hagar ran off into the desert thus threatening her survival.

It was in this desperate situation that an angel met her and told her to return and submit to Sarah. She was also given a promise that her unborn child would have descendants *too numerous to count* (Genesis 16:10).

Hagar referred to God as *the God who sees me* (16:13), but had she disobeyed the angel she would most likely have perished. Now encouraged by this knowledge of God's concern for her and her unborn son, she returned to Sarah.

Reflection: *What a difference it makes in facing a difficult situation to know that God is the One who sees me. Going back instead of continuing to run away is never easy, but it can be the way to know God's protection and blessing.*

GOD ALMIGHTY—EL SHADDAI
(Genesis 17:1)

THE NAME *GOD ALMIGHTY* is a reminder that he is an omnipotent and all sufficient God. The name is first mentioned in Genesis 17. It had been twenty-four years since God promised Abraham that his descendants would become a great nation (12:2), and now Abraham was ninety-nine years of age and Sarah his wife was ninety.

God had allowed Abraham and Sarah to go well beyond the normal age of child bearing in order to test their faith in him. God now appeared to Abraham as *God Almighty* (17:1), confirming his covenant, and saying that Sarah would bear a child within a year, (7:21).

Reflection: *Trusting God is often not easy, especially when it seems that the situation is impossible. The good news is that "God Almighty" is patient and does not give up on us. Abraham was "fully persuaded that God had power to do what he had promised" (Romans 4:21). We too need to trust "God Almighty" to complete his purposes in our lives.*

THE EVERLASTING AND ETERNAL GOD—EL OLAM
(Isaiah 40:28)

WE ARE ALL FINITE creatures, subject to changes in our circumstances and limited to one locality at a time. There are limits to our knowledge and understanding, and we are subject to the laws of nature. Eventually we all die.

By contrast, God exists both within his creation and outside of it. He is not affected by change and he is present everywhere. He has all knowledge and his power is unlimited. As the *Everlasting and Eternal God* he enjoys an endless and perfect existence.

Isaiah 40:28–29, indicates that the *Everlasting God . . . gives strength to the weary . . . and power to the weak*. Verse 31 concludes that we should therefore, *hope in the Lord, be renewed in strength, soar on wings like eagles* and *run and not grow weary*.

Reflection: *"To soar" and "to run" are images of a person who is able to continue even in difficult circumstances. Therefore knowing God as Everlasting and Eternal makes all the difference in being able to persevere.*

Names for, and References to, God the Father

THE GOD OF BETHEL
(Genesis 31:13)

BETHEL, MEANS "HOUSE OF God" and was the place where God revealed himself to Abraham, promising to give the land to his offspring (Genesis, 12:78). Jacob too had slept there and God had renewed this promise to him. Jacob had made a vow to own the Lord as his God, to make the site a place of worship and to give a tenth of what he owned to the Lord, (28:22).

The years passed and again God spoke, but this time as *the God of Bethel*, to remind Jacob of his vow and telling him to return to his homeland.

To hear again the voice of the Lord and to have the memory of Bethel drawn to his attention must have been a defining moment in setting the future course of his life.

Reflection: *Is there a "Bethel" where the Lord spoke to you and where you made your promises to him? Perhaps like Jacob, there are still some promises that need to be fulfilled by you.*

GOD, THE GOD OF ISRAEL—EL ELOHE ISRAEL
(Genesis 33:20)

JACOB HAD FIRST TRICKED his brother Esau by getting him to sell his birthright (Genesis 25:29–34), and then escaped from his brother who wanted to kill him (27:41). Now, twenty years later, he was returning home (32:7).

Hoping to appease his brother's anger he sent a gift of animals ahead of him, but that night at Peniel he wrestled with a stranger. At daybreak he learned that he has been wrestling with God and that his name would now be changed to Israel (32:28).

The meeting of the brothers was an occasion of great joy as they reconciled to each other. Jacob continued his journey, purchased land and erected an altar, calling it, *God, the God of Israel* after the name he had been given. Jacob was now able to make a fresh start in worshipping his God in this renewed relationship.

Reflection: *Restoring broken relationships with others is always a prerequisite to worship and in having a personal relationship with God (Matthew 5:24).*

THE MIGHTY ONE OF JACOB
(Genesis 49:24-25)

The Mighty One of Jacob was a title that resulted from Jacob's lifetime experiences of God's faithfulness. Jacob still remembered the details of God's covenant, to bless him and his descendants (Genesis 28:13-15). There were also occasions when either the angels or God himself appeared to him, reassuring him of his presence and blessing, (Genesis 32:1, 2; 22-30; 35:9-12).

Through these dealings with God and his experiences of life, Jacob had grown in his knowledge and confidence in him. Therefore, in blessing his son Joseph before he died he was able to personalize the name of God by emphasizing his relationship with him as *the Mighty One of Jacob*.

Later King David also used this title, *the Mighty One of Jacob*, to refer to God (Psalm 132:2, 5) as did the prophet Isaiah, (Isaiah 60:16; 49:26).

Reflection: *Through this title, "the Mighty One of Jacob", he identified himself with God. What intimacy in fellowship is also possible for us as we grow in our knowledge of Him?*

THE LORD WHO HEALS YOU—YHWH ROPHI
(Exodus 15:26)

"The LORD who heals you" was the name revealed by God to Moses at the waters of Marah. The Israelites had been delivered from slavery in Egypt and for three days had traveled without water to drink (Exodus 15:22-23).

Now they started to grumble when they found that the water at Marah was bitter. Moses therefore prayed and God showed him a piece of wood that he threw into the water and miraculously the water became sweet.

The Lord assured Moses that if the people obeyed him, then he would keep them free from the diseases of the Egyptians. The Lord then told Moses his name: *I am the LORD who heals you*.

Reflection: *The occasion above indicated that God's protection from sickness was equally as important as being healed from a disease. Remember, it is the Lord who can keep us healthy, heal the broken hearted (Psalm 147:3), forgive all our iniquities, and heal all our diseases, (Psalm 103:3).*

THE LORD WILL PROVIDE—YHWH JIREH
Genesis 22:14

It must have been a difficult decision for Abraham to obey when God asked him to offer his son Isaac as a sacrifice on Mt. Moriah. If he sacrificed his only son, he would no longer have descendants that God could bless. However, Abraham's faith was now strong as he believed his son would be raised from the dead. (Hebrews 11:19)

As he was about to kill his son God spoke and stopped him, providing a ram nearby which Abraham sacrificed as a substitute for his son. Amazed at God's last minute provision, Abraham gave the place this name in memory of God's goodness: *The LORD Will Provide*, (Genesis 22:14).

Abraham had demonstrated his obedience and God now renewed his promise to bless him and multiply his descendants.

Reflection: *There will be occasions when God will challenge you to give up something you value. When you trust and obey him in these circumstances you too will see the evidence of his name, "The Lord Will Provide".*

THE LORD IS MY BANNER—YHWH NISSI
Exodus 17:15

The Israelites had recently left Egypt where they had been slaves, but as they traveled they were watched by the Amalekites, who cut off the stragglers and then fronted up for a full scale battle. It must have been a terrifying occasion, for the Israelites had not been trained to fight, but Joshua chose an army while Moses took the staff of God and went with Hur and Aaron to the top of the hill.

As Moses held the staff aloft with the help of Hur and Aaron so Joshua won the battle. Scripture records that Joshua had overcome the Amalekites with the sword, but Moses knew that the victory had been due to the staff of God being raised as their banner. (Exodus 17:12-13). The staff had been a symbol of God's presence, his power and his authority.

Reflection: *With the Lord as your Banner, you too can pray knowing that the Lord can give you victory against the power of the evil one.*

THE LORD, WHOSE NAME IS JEALOUS
(Exodus 34:14)

WE USUALLY THINK OF jealousy as a negative emotion and list it along with other sins of our human nature (Galatians 5:19–20). But jealousy also has a positive meaning, and thirteen times in the Old Testament God is referred to as a jealous God.

In this positive sense, jealousy indicates the intensity of God's love and is among a small group of names used by the LORD. This name *Jealous* was revealed to Moses on the occasion when he went to the top of Mt. Sinai with two tablets of stone in order to get a second copy of the law (Exodus 34).

The LORD then declared his character as a *compassionate and gracious God* (34:6), and told Moses to destroy the heathen worship practices. They were *not to worship any other God, for the LORD, whose name is Jealous, is a jealous God* (34:14).

Reflection: *What are the implications for your relationship with the Lord, knowing that his name is Jealous?*

MY PRESENCE
"My Presence will go with you" (Exodus 33:14).

THE LORD CALLED ISRAEL a *stiff necked people* because of their behavior in worshipping the golden calf (Exodus 32). He then told Moses that an angel would go ahead to drive out the enemies from the land (33:2). Moses was clearly concerned that the Lord should ask him to lead the people with only the presence of an angel and therefore he pleaded his case before the Lord, (33:13–16). In reply the Lord said, *My Presence will go with you and I will give you rest*, (33:14).

The expression *My Presence* means literally "my face" and personifies the Lord as watching over him. In the years that followed, Moses was to prove the Lord's faithfulness on many occasions, knowing the experience of his *Presence*.

Reflection: *The assurance that "my Presence" will go with you, was a promise to Moses, but there was a more complete fulfillment when the Holy Spirit came to the believers at Pentecost. Now all believers enjoy his presence.*

THE COMPASSIONATE AND GRACIOUS GOD
(Exodus 34:6)

ON THE SECOND OCCASION that Moses ascended Mt. Sinai to receive the Commandments, God revealed himself using this descriptive expansion of his name: *the LORD, the LORD the compassionate and gracious God*. The words that follow this announcement indicate the nature of his compassion and grace and the practical ways that he would show his love towards his people.

It was a transforming experience for Moses to meet the Lord on Sinai and to learn the nature of his compassion and grace. *Slow to anger, abounding in love and faithfulness, maintaining love and forgiving wickedness*. Their Lord was none other than the *God of love*, (2 Corinthians 13:11).

Reflection: *Moses was not immediately aware of the change, but when he spoke with his people his face was radiant and had to be covered (Ex.34:33). We too "with unveiled faces all reflect the Lord's glory, and are being transformed into his likeness with ever-increasing glory, which comes from the Lord, who is the Spirit" (2 Corinthians 3:18).*

A MERCIFUL GOD
For the LORD your God is a merciful God (Deuteronomy 4:31)

THE ULTIMATE EVIDENCE THAT the Lord is a *merciful God* was seen when he established his new covenant through sending his Son as the atoning sacrifice *for our sins* (1 John 2:2). Knowing that God will keep the terms of his covenant helps us to understand the nature of his mercy.

When Jesus was on earth some people sought his help. For instance, the Canaanite woman cried desperately, *"Lord, Son of David, have mercy on me!"* (Matthew 15:22). Invariably Jesus responded to such requests and brought help and healing.

Knowing that God will keep his covenant through Christ should be an encouragement to trust our merciful God. *Let us then approach the throne of grace with confidence, so that we may receive mercy and find grace to help us in our time of need*, (Hebrews 4:16).

Reflection: *Experiencing the blessings of a merciful God obligates us to be merciful to others. "Freely you have received, freely give" (Matthew 10:8b).*

THE LORD WHO MAKES YOU HOLY—M'QUADDISHKHEM
(Leviticus 20:7-8)

Moses was told that the people had to consecrate themselves and be holy by obeying the law. The word "consecrate" and the words "makes you holy" have similar meanings and have the idea of being set apart for God and his purposes.

The people had to live holy lives, but it was the LORD who had chosen them from the time of Abraham, that made them a holy nation, (Deuteronomy 7:6-7). As God's holy people, the behavior of Israel often did not match their standing as the people of God, for they failed to show God's holiness to the nations around them.

God therefore had to provide his Son to die for the sin of the world in order to demonstrate that he was *the LORD who makes you holy.*

Reflection: *"For he chose us in him before the creation of the world to be holy" (Ephesians 1:4). Now that we enjoy the life of Christ, we are empowered by the Spirit to "be holy".*

THE GOD OF JESHURUN
(Deuteronomy 33:26-27)

In the blessing given by Moses before he died he referred to the *God of Jeshurun*. The name conveys the idea of Israel as a morally upright people in an endearing relationship with their God. The *God of Jeshurun* is therefore a God who loves his people and is seen to be ever watchful over them, providing *refuge* in time of trouble and carrying them in his *everlasting arms*.

Later Isaiah contrasted the names of Jacob and Jeshurun (44:2), reminding Israel of its willfulness, in contrast to their relationship with God as his holy people.

Israel was chosen by God from the time of Abraham as God's people to worship and obey him so that his glory would be seen through them by the surrounding nations.

Reflection: *Like Jeshurun, we too are the people of God as we have become the spiritual children of Abraham, (Galatians 3:7). But now we have a better covenant relationship, for through Christ we enjoy the Spirit's presence and power in our lives.*

GOD OF Gods AND LORD OF Lords
(Deuteronomy 10:17)

When Israel first received the Commandments they knew that God would not abide his people worshipping false gods, (Exodus 20:5). They knew that God's laws were for their *own good* (Deuteronomy 10:13), and so they were to separate themselves from evil and obey the requirements of the law (10:16). They were to *fear* (revere) the *Lord . . . and serve him* (10:20).

Moses knew that the ultimate inspiration to worship and service would come from an understanding and contemplation of the LORD (YHWH).

By contrast, the other nations worshiped and sought to appease their petty deities, but the God of Israel was *God of gods and Lord of lords*. In other words he was Sovereign ruler, *mighty and awesome* with authority over all creation and could not be bribed.

Reflection: *Knowing the awesome greatness of our God and the covenant relationship we have with him should help us give priority to what is really important in life:–our worship and our obedient service for our Lord.*

THE LORD OF ALL THE EARTH
(Joshua 3:11)

The Israelites could not enter the land of Canaan because the Jordan River was in flood. Therefore the Lord told Joshua that the priests should carry the *Ark* and stand in the shallows at the water's edge (3:8).

Joshua then referred to the Ark as the *Ark of the Covenant of the Lord of all the earth* (3:11). The Lord then blocked off the river upstream so that the people could walk across the dry riverbed (3:17).

Much later the Psalmist also celebrated the *Lord of all the earth* when he described the Lord's control of the environment for the people to see his glory, (Psalm 97:2–6). The prophet Zechariah also spoke of the *Lord of all the earth,* as demonstrating his control over the affairs of men, (Zechariah 4:14).

Reflection: *Whether it is the physical environment, the affairs of the nations or the doing of God's work, he is in control, for he is "Lord of all the earth".*

THE LORD IS PEACE—YHWH SHALOM
(Judges 6:24)

God had allowed Israel to be invaded continually by the Midianites because of their wrongdoings (Judges 6:1–7). It was only after they cried to the Lord for help that an angel from the LORD appeared to Gideon.

Gideon was terrified, but he was told to be at peace (6:23). In response, Gideon built an altar to the Lord calling it . . . *The LORD is Peace.*

In the events that followed, Gideon was instrumental in destroying the heathen worship of Baal and with God's guiding, selected a small army of three hundred men to fight and defeat the Midianites. Peace was now restored to Israel during the remaining forty years of Gideon's lifetime (8:28).

Reflection: *God had given Gideon the blessing of peace (6:23), but a battle had to be fought before peace was restored. For us Christ has won the battle against sin and death, but we too have to fight a battle against the spiritual powers of darkness, (Ephesians 6:12).*

THE LORD ALMIGHTY, THE LORD OF HOSTS/ARMIES—YHWH SABAOTH
(1 Samuel 1:3)

When Elkanah and his wife Hannah went up to Shiloh to sacrifice to the *LORD Almighty,* Hannah was hurting bitterly because she had no children. She therefore prayed and made a vow to *the LORD Almighty* promising that if he gave her a son, she would dedicate him to the service of the Lord (1:11). The Lord later granted her request and so she brought her child Samuel to serve at the temple (1:24).

Later, the Israelites thought superstitiously that if they went into battle against the Philistines and took with them the *ark of the covenant of the LORD Almighty* (4:4), then the Lord would help them defeat the Philistines. The result was a disaster, for they not only lost the battle but the Ark was taken from them.

Reflection: *Note the contrasting attitudes of these people to the LORD Almighty. Understanding the position and authority of the LORD should help us guard against ever trying to manipulate him.*

A GOD WHO KNOWS
(1 Samuel 2:3)

THE TITLE "A GOD who knows" occurs in the song of thanks that Hannah offered to God when she presented her young son Samuel at the temple. Hannah was aware that God knew all about her circumstances.

God's knowledge about Hannah was perfect and complete because as God, he exists both within and beyond his creation and is not limited by time and space. His knowledge is not only quantitatively different from ours in terms of the volume of his knowledge, but also qualitatively different.

His knowledge extends beyond the event itself, to its causes, its consequences and the motives of the people involved. He sees events from the perspective of eternity. Therefore events in the past, the present or the future, are seen with equal vividness.

Reflection: *"Nothing in all creation is hidden from God's sight . . . to whom we must give account" (Hebrews 4:13). Living in relationship with the "God who knows", should be a source of comfort and an incentive to holy living.*

THE GLORY OF ISRAEL
(1 Samuel 15:29)

A NATION'S GLORY is often seen in its sporting heroes, in its literary and scientific achievements, through its military strength and in its economic power. In Old Testament times Israel had no glory of this type, but they had God who had covenanted to bless them. He was *the Glory of Israel*, the One who would be their glory.

God's glory was associated with his presence and his person and when he revealed himself to his people it was always in the context of his glory, (e.g. Exodus 16:10, 11; Deuteronomy 5:24; Isaiah 6:3; Ezekiel 1:27, 28)

But God wanted the nations to see his glory through his people. If they would live holy lives and worship him, *then all the peoples on earth will see that you are called by the name of the Lord* (Deuteronomy 28:10).

Reflection: *God continues to display his glory through the splendor of his creation and the holiness of his people. Pray that others will see his glory revealed through you.*

MY STRONGHOLD, MY REFUGE, MY SAVIOR
(2 Samuel 22:3)

DAVID REFERRED TO THE Lord as *my Stronghold, my Refuge, my Savior,* indicating that he knew the Lord had saved his life from his enemy King Saul. The title as a metaphor pictures God's care of David as being like a fortified city that gave protection to him and his friends.

But in ancient times the strongholds of Canaan had to be destroyed if Israel was to conquer and occupy the land. For instance, we read that King Og's realm consisted of sixty cities and *all these cities were fortified with high walls and with gates and bars* (Deuteronomy 3:5). The best known of the fortified cities of Canaan was Jericho and its destruction is recorded in Joshua 6:2–25.

Reflection: *"The Lord is the stronghold of my life, of whom shall I be afraid?" (Psalm 27:1).* Life can be a struggle but we can know that the *"Lord is faithful. He will establish you and guard you against the evil one"* (2 Thessalonians 3:3).

MY LAMP
You are my lamp, O LORD; the LORD turns my darkness into light,
(2 Samuel 22:29).

AN EARLY JEWISH LAMP was similar in appearance to a teapot without its lid. The open bowl held the olive oil and on one side there was a spout with a wick of dried flax, while on the other side there was a small handle.

Unlike lamps today that can shine a beam of light, an oil lamp only gave light to the area immediately around it. Throughout the Bible the lamp is used as a symbol of light and in the above verse David used this image as a descriptive metaphor of the Lord.

For the Lord to be described as *my Lamp,* indicated David was conscious of the Lord's guidance.

Reflection: *Knowing the Lord as a Lamp means that his word, "is a lamp to my feet and a light for my path" (Psalm 119:105). Also, as a Lamp, nothing lies hidden from the Lord for he knows our motives, thoughts and actions.*

Names for, and References to, God the Father

GOD OVER ALL THE KINGDOMS OF THE EARTH
(2 Kings 19:15)

King Hezekiah received a letter from the King of Assyria warning him that his God could not protect his people from the might of the Assyrian army. On receiving the letter, Hezekiah immediately took it to the temple and prayed, (Isaiah 37:14–15).

For Hezekiah to refer to the Lord as, *"God over all the kingdoms of the earth"*, indicated that as creator he had *made heaven and the earth* (2 Kings 19:15) and was in control of all things. Hezekiah was confident to pray and expect God to protect them against the might of the Assyrian army.

That night the angel of the Lord killed 185,000 men of the Assyrians (19:35), thus demonstrating the truth that *God cannot be mocked* (Galatians 6:7).

Reflection: *In the most difficult of circumstances we can still come to the Lord and acknowledge him as "God over all". We can be assured that he is present with us and able to work on our behalf for his glory.*

THE GOD OF HEAVEN
(Nehemiah 1:5)

The title, the LORD, *God of heaven,* was used by Nehemiah when he prayed to God about the devastation of the Jerusalem city wall. The title was also used to record the formal declaration releasing the Jews from Babylon (Ezra 1:2) and in a personal letter to Ezra from the king (Ezra 7:12). It was the *God of heaven* who was acknowledged as the all-powerful God of Israel.

For us today God is more than just the *God of heaven,* for Jesus said *you may be sons of your Father in heaven* (Matthew 5:45) and he taught his disciples to pray to *Our Father in heaven,* (Matthew 6:9).

It was to heaven that Jesus returned when he *sat down at the right hand of the Majesty in heaven* (Hebrews 1:3), there to prepare a place for us (John 14:2).

Reflection: *The "Lord God of heaven" is the "Majesty of heaven" who is "our Father in heaven." What a relationship we have with him through Christ.*

THE GREAT AND AWESOME GOD
(Nehemiah 1:5)

THERE ARE FOUR OCCASIONS in the Bible where God is referred to as a *great and awesome God*. In Deuteronomy 7:21, God's people were told not to be terrified by their enemies *for the LORD your God, who is among you, is a great and awesome God*.

Then in Nehemiah 1:5, and 9:32, and in Daniel 9:4, this descriptive title of the Lord is presented in the context of his covenant love for his people. In each of these references he is seen as faithful in protecting them.

As a *great* God he is preeminent, but the word *awesome* can also be translated "fearsome". Israel was therefore to know their God as preeminent in power and authority, while being feared and respected through their obedience.

Reflection: *We too have been brought into a covenant relationship with God our Father through Jesus our Lord. We therefore need to show our fear of him too through our reverence, our worship and our obedience.*

THE ONE ENTHRONED IN HEAVEN
(Psalm 2:4)

THE *ONE ENTHRONED IN* heaven, is a title for God that refers to him as deserving of all honor and as having supreme authority and power to reign. In the Psalm above, there is a contrast between his kingly rule and the kings and rulers of the earth who *take their stand . . . against the Lord* (2:2).

The laughter and scorn of the *One enthroned in heaven* (2:4), changes to rebuke and anger as he terrifies the nations in his wrath (2:5) and rules them *with an iron scepter* (2:9). The psalm therefore has a future fulfillment, for these words are also descriptive of Christ's triumphant reign recorded in Revelation 12:10 and 19:15 when he will rule the nations of the earth.

The *One enthroned in heaven* is therefore the God whose plans will not be frustrated and who will come in judgment against those who oppose him.

Reflection: *Today we enthrone him in our lives as we acknowledge him as our Lord and our God.*

MY KING AND MY GOD
(Psalm 5:2)

THERE ARE THREE PSALMS in which this title for God accompanies a cry from the heart of the writers. The title indicates that God had kingly authority over their lives and, in acknowledging him as *"my God"*, they affirm their devotion to him.

The title also implies a relationship with God in which they have the confidence to pray for their needs, knowing that he will hear their prayers. In Psalm 5 David knew that his enemies were seeking his downfall and so he came before the Lord in worship (5:8).

In Psalm 44 there is a cry for help on behalf of the nation after a defeat by the enemy (44:26) and Psalm 84 is the cry of a distant traveler who longed to get to Jerusalem and worship the Lord at the temple (84:3).

Reflection: *What a privilege it is to know the Lord as "my King and my God" and that he hears our prayers as we worship and serve him.*

O LORD OUR LORD
O LORD, our Lord, how majestic is your name in all the earth, (Psalm 8:1, 9).

PSALM 8 BEGINS AND ends with this beautiful expression of worship in which the LORD (YHWH), the self-existent God who is unchanging in his nature, is addressed as our Lord (Adon) or Master.

The mention of "your name" is a reference to the character of the Lord and throughout the Psalm David highlights the majestic greatness of the name of our LORD through the glory of his creation.

Read the psalm and note how the description of creation and the beauty of the heavens is contrasted with God's creation of men and women. Note also how man is defined in relation to the angels (8:5), to each other (8:2, 5) and to creation (8:6–8).

Reflection: *To worship the LORD as "our Lord" means acting responsibly to care for the creation, and to treat people with dignity and compassion.*

THE PRAISE OF ISRAEL
(Psalm 22:3)

THE IMPORTANCE OF ANYTHING is often reflected in the richness of vocabulary used to describe it. The Hebrew language illustrates this fact by the vocabulary used to praise God.

- There was an *offering of praise (hillulim)* to the Lord (Leviticus 19:24).
- Joshua advised Achan to give *praise (toda)* through confession and thanksgiving (Joshua 7:19).
- The joyful playing of instruments indicated *instruments of praise (oz)* (2 Chronicles 30:21b).
- Singing was a feature of Israel's praise. David said, *I will sing praise (zamar) to your name* (Psalm 9:2).
- Praise was centered on God for he was *the Praise (tehilla) of Israel* (Psalm 22:3).
- David expressed his gratitude to the Lord, *praise (yadda) his holy name* (Psalm 30:4).
- David also exalted the Lord. *The LORD lives! Praise (barak) be to my Rock* (Psalm 18:46).
- David exalted the Lord over other gods. *For great is the LORD and most worthy of praise (halal).* (1 Chron.16:25).

Reflection: *Seek to live your life for his Praise.*

MY ROCK, MY FORTRESS AND MY DELIVERER
(Psalm 18:2)

IN THIS DESCRIPTIVE TITLE for God David rejoices in God's goodness in protecting him from his enemy King Saul. The title gives us a picture of how David felt about God.

As *"my Rock"*, the Lord brought stability, strength and permanence to him in a time of uncertainty when his life was being threatened. As *"my Fortress"*, God was a place of refuge, a stronghold and a place of protection. As *"my Deliverer"*, the Lord proved himself faithful in helping him defeat his enemy. Terms in the psalm such as "rescue", "save", "enemies scattered" and "routed" all refer to the Lord's loving intervention.

David used the same descriptive title for God in 2 Sam.22:2, when again he sang praises to the Lord for his deliverance (22:50).

Reflection: *God was not some distant deity to David but rather an ever-present help in trouble (Psalm 46:1). May we too in the journey of life experience our God as "my Rock, my Fortress, and my Deliverer".*

MY SHIELD AND THE HORN OF MY SALVATION, MY STRONGHOLD
(Psalm 18:2)

IN PSALM 18 THERE is a cluster of seven titles referring to God that identify him as David's protector. Altogether these titles provide a comprehensive picture of this protection.

The Shield gave protection from the arrows of the enemy and from the sword in close-up combat. As *"my Shield"* David had experienced the Lord's protection on many occasions.

Just as the horn of an animal is a symbol of its strength and power, so David knew God as "the Horn of my Salvation". David knew that he could rely on the strength and power of the Lord to save him from his enemies.

The third image of the "Stronghold" indicates a defensive fortress where people would be safe from enemy attack. David had experienced times when God had given him a safe place to hide.

Reflection: *In the spiritual battles of life we too need to know the Lord as "my Shield, and the Horn of my Salvation, my Stronghold".*

THE KING OF GLORY

Who is he, this King of Glory?
The LORD Almighty—he is the King of Glory, (Psalm 24:10).

JERUSALEM THE FORTRESS HAD become the City of David (2 Samuel 5:9), but many years passed before the Ark was finally brought to the city. Its arrival was a grand occasion and Psalm 24 was written by David to either celebrate or commemorate this event.

The arrival of the Ark symbolized the coming of the *King of glory* to the Tabernacle of David. *Lift up your heads, O you gates* (24:7) was the King's poetic call personifying the gates and calling on them to be ready to welcome the *King of glory*. Whereas worship at the Tabernacle at Gibeon had been centered on sacrifice, now at the Tabernacle of David a new dimension of celebration was added, (Psalm 149:3).

Reflection: *To worship the King of glory will include celebration, but it must always include confession of sin, for worship is intended for those who have "clean hands and a pure heart" (Psalm 24:4).*

THE GOD OF GLORY

. . . the God of Glory thunders (Psalm 29:3)

As the above verse indicates, the *God of glory* is seen in his creation, and therefore our response should be to *ascribe to the LORD the glory due his name* (29:2).

This descriptive title, *the God of glory,* was also used by Stephen when he made his defense before the Jewish leaders and said that the "*God of glory*" had appeared to Abraham when he called him to leave his homeland (Acts 7:1–3). Abraham's vision of the *God of glory* meant that he was ready to obey his call.

For the Israelites the glory of the presence of God was seen in the cloud that covered the Tabernacle by day and then appeared as fire by night (Exodus 13:21–22). The High Priest too was conscious of the glory of God's presence in the Holy of Holies, (Leviticus 16:2).

Reflection: *Today the God of Glory is still seen in his creation, in his Word, and in his people—the Church.*

MY SHEPHERD

(Psalm 23:1)

David saw himself in a similar relationship to the Lord as sheep are to their shepherd. So he spoke of the Lord personally as *my Shepherd*. The Psalm starts and finishes with the name of the Lord and it is for the sake of his name (23:3) that he takes responsibility for us.

The role of the Shepherd is outlined through seven activities in verses two to five. These include occasions when he makes us rest, when he leads us, when he restores us, when he guides us, when he comforts us, when he provides for us and when he anoints us.

We experience this help in both the good times, when we are refreshed in *green pastures,* as well as in the tough experiences of life. Food prepared *in the presence of our enemies* (23:5), is an invitation to enjoy his provision in spite of difficult circumstances.

Reflection: *In both the good and bad experiences of life remember "the LORD is my Shepherd, I shall not want".*

Names for, and References to, God the Father

MY LIGHT, MY SALVATION, MY STRONGHOLD
(Psalm 27:1)

IN THE OPENING VERSES of Psalm 27 David expressed supreme confidence in his Lord to guide and guard him throughout his life. Because of his relationship with his Lord he could say, *the Lord is my light and my salvation whom shall I fear? The Lord is the stronghold of my life of whom shall I be afraid?*

On three occasions David had been anointed king, (1 Samuel 16:13; 2 Samuel 2:4; 5:3), and from the first occasion *the Spirit of the Lord came upon David in power* (1 Samuel 16:13).

Later, the Lord gave David covenant promises that he would be a great king, (2 Samuel 7:8–16). David's greatness as a king was therefore not based on confidence in his own ability. Rather, he had the knowledge and encouragement of the Lord's promises and blessings.

Reflection: *Today we too have every reason to have our confidence in the Lord and to say, "the Lord is my light and my salvation ... the stronghold of my life".*

THE LORD STRONG AND MIGHTY, THE LORD MIGHTY IN BATTLE
(Psalm 24:8)

IN PSALM 24, DAVID identified the *King of Glory* by the two descriptive titles that speak of his greatness. Firstly, as *the "LORD strong and mighty"*, he saw the Creation as the Lord's, for he said *the earth is the Lord's, and everything in it* (24:1). Then, to this description of strength and might he adds "the *LORD mighty in battle*". He is now thinking of the Lord's help in his recent military victories.

By this time David had become a great king, but he humbly recognized that it was the Lord who had helped him win his victories and so deserved his devotion and worship.

Reflection: *The "Lord strong and mighty, the LORD mighty in battle" demonstrated his power in his creation and proved himself faithful to David in the struggles of life. He will do the same for us also. We therefore need to worship him as David did, with humility of spirit, integrity of heart and an upright lifestyle.*

THE RULER OF ALL THINGS
(1 Chronicles 29:12)

A RULER IS SOMEONE who governs or judges, and in the Bible the word has the idea of being first in order by rank. God therefore has this position and authority as *the Ruler of all things*.

In 1 Chronicles 29:10–13, King David had prayed before the assembly of his people, worshipping the Lord for his greatness and acknowledging God's strength and power as *Ruler of all things* (29:11–12).

The people had been generous in giving towards the costs of building the Temple and now David was about to hand over his rule as King to his Son Solomon. David was concerned that the nation along with Solomon should continue to be wholehearted in their devotion to the Lord. (29:14–18).

Reflection: *God as "ruler of all things" continues to have all authority and power. It is his world, and so we, like the people of David's day, should be wholehearted in our devotion to the Lord.*

THE GOD OF TRUTH
(Psalm 31:5)

IN THIS PSALM DAVID records his cry to the Lord as there were people plotting to take his life (31:13). David was being treated unfairly, so he appealed for deliverance (redemption) on the basis of the Lord's righteousness (31:1).

As God's chosen leader he knew that the honor of the Lord's name was involved, for he said, *for the sake of your name lead and guide me* (31:3). Then, in dependence on the Lord he committed himself to God. *Into your hands I commit my spirit* (31:5). David was able to entrust his life to the Lord because he knew him as the *God of truth*.

The word *truth* means more than the idea that God is truthful. To know the *God of truth* is to be absolutely confident that he is faithful and reliable.

Reflection: *"Into your hands I commit my spirit" were David's words that were repeated by Jesus on the cross, (Luke 23:46). We too need to entrust our lives to "the God of truth".*

MY HIDING PLACE
(Psalm 32:7)

IN THE EXPRESSION *My Hiding Place*, David expresses his confidence that, having confessed his sin, the Lord would protect him from trouble so that in the midst of danger he could rejoice.

The Hebrew word for *hiding place* is also translated *shelter*. In Psalm 91:1 we read, *he who dwells in the shelter of the Most High will rest in the shadow of the Almighty*. The Lord as our *hiding place* is therefore our protecting shelter.

As our *hiding place* the Lord should not be thought of as a place to which we retreat as hermits. Rather, in the midst of life, like David, we need to confess our sin to the Lord and learn to rejoice as we enjoy the Lord's shelter and protection.

Reflection: *"Rejoice in the Lord always" (Philippians 4:4). The degree to which you can rejoice in the midst of difficulties is a measure of the degree to which you know the protecting shelter of the Lord as your "hiding place".*

THE KING OF ALL THE EARTH
(Psalm 47:7)

UNLIKE THE NATIONS AROUND Israel who had kings, Israel needed no such person, for God was their king, (Deuteronomy 33:5).

But the time came when Israel wanted their own king in order to be like the nations, (Deuteronomy 17:14-20). In wanting a king, God told Samuel that they had rejected him as their king (1 Samuel 8:7). The kings of Israel and Judah often worshipped foreign gods and their misrule reflected their rejection of God as their king.

One bright spot in this sad history was the recognition by King David of God's absolute authority as King and his submission to him as the one to be worshipped. For instance the Psalmist said, *You are my King and my God* (Psalm 44:4).

Reflection: *Being King of all the earth also means that the kings of the earth belong to God (Psalm 47:9). One day all nations will come and worship before the "Lord God Almighty . . . the King of the ages" (Revelation 15:3, 4).*

MY STRENGTH, MY FORTRESS, MY LOVING GOD
(Psalm 59:9, 17)

This composite title occurs twice in this psalm and indicates King David's experience in knowing God. He was confident that God loved him and therefore he felt secure in his role as King. On this occasion his enemies were seeking his downfall, but he knew God as a *Loving God* who would be his *Fortress* giving him the protection he needed.

King David was quick to acknowledge that the Lord would answer his cry for help and as *My Strength* he overcame his enemies, exercising strong military leadership and extending the borders of the Kingdom of Israel. Today the Star of David is featured on the flag of Israel in his honor.

Reflection: *Be strong in the Lord (Ephesians 6:10). Christians should be able to look to the Lord as David did and say, "My Strength, my fortress, my loving God". Therefore, in the difficulties and uncertainties of life we should remember that "those who hope in the Lord will renew their strength" (Isaiah 40:31).*

A FATHER TO THE FATHERLESS, A DEFENDER OF WIDOWS
(Psalm 68:4, 5)

In Old Testament times when a father died this usually meant that close relatives would need to help the bereaved family.

However, for such families life was often tough and some families became destitute and family members had to sell themselves into slavery. Nevertheless, God had made it clear that Israel was not to exploit the less fortunate in society.

He said, *Do not take advantage of a widow or an orphan* (Exodus 22:22). *Do not deprive the alien or the fatherless of justice, or take the cloak of a widow as a pledge* (Deuteronomy 24:17). God would be a *Father to the fatherless, a defender of widows,* but the nation also had to act responsibly in caring for these people in need.

Reflection: *We too have a responsibility to care for one another, but it is comforting to know that, as our Heavenly Father, we should cast all our anxiety on him because he cares for us (1 Peter 5:6–7).*

THE SHEPHERD OF ISRAEL
(Psalm 80:1)

Shepherds and sheep were familiar sights in Palestine during Bible times. The size of a flock was an indication of a man's wealth and the sheep provided an important source of food and income.

Quality lambs were always in demand for sacrifices at the Temple. In a land with limited rainfall and with no fences to confine the sheep, the role of the shepherd was important.

Sheep had to be led to places where there was sufficient grass to sustain them and then guarded throughout the day from wild animals or from wandering away and getting lost. Sheep and shepherds therefore provided a rich imagery that was suited to illustrate Israel's character and God's relationship with his people.

Reflection: *Knowing how the "Shepherd of Israel" was faithful in caring for his people in the past, should give us confidence to call on him as our Shepherd to guide and protect us. We should pray this way too for the persecuted Church around the world.*

THE GOD WHO SAVES ME
(Psalm 88:1)

For one of the sons of Korah, life was a bewildering experience. He speaks of *the God who saves me,* but for him there was no deliverance. He therefore concludes that his problems are due to God's wrath, (88:7), and his recourse is to cry to the Lord in prayer (88:13–14). What makes the Psalm significant is that the writer, in spite of his anguish, never doubts who God is.

We need to remember that suffering is part of life in a sinful and imperfect world, but the Lord may use a time of suffering to bring people closer to himself, (Revelation 3:19). In such circumstances God is acting in love towards them and not in wrath. Therefore, they *suffer according to God's will* (1 Peter 4:19).

Reflection: *Aspects of suffering are a mystery, but we can take encouragement in Paul's words, "My grace is sufficient for you, for my power is made perfect in weakness" (2 Corinthians 12:9).*

THE LORD OUR MAKER
(Psalm 95:6)

THE TITLE REMINDS US we do not exist by chance and Genesis tells us that we were made in God's image and likeness (Genesis 1:26). This means that we were made more like our Creator than the rest of creation and given a dignity to our being and a purpose to our existence.

Knowing who our Maker is should also satisfy us that we are made as he intended us to be and that we should develop and use the abilities he has given to us. The implication is that we are responsible to our Maker for the way we live our lives.

Thinking about our origin and existence should lead us to worship the *LORD our Maker*. This was the attitude of the Psalmist when he said, *Come let us bow down in worship, let us kneel before the Lord our Maker* (Psalm 95:6).

Reflection: *We read that people had forgotten the Lord as their Maker (Isaiah 51:12–13). Worshipping the Lord will save us from this misfortune.*

MY GOD THE ROCK
(Psalm 94:22)

THE REFERENCE TO GOD as a *Rock* occurs around thirty times in the Old Testament and conveys the meaning of his protection, strength and security. It suggests the idea of someone on whom you can depend. Several people in the Old Testament speak of God in this way.

Jacob gave Joseph a blessing that would enable him to withstand his enemies because . . . *the Shepherd, the Rock of Israel* would help and bless him (Genesis 49:24). Hannah had proved God's faithfulness when he gave her a child. Now at the Temple she prays–*there is no Rock like our God* (1 Samuel 2:2).

In several of the Psalms David praised God as *the Rock of our Salvation* (95:1); *the rock in whom I take refuge* (94:22); *my Father, my God, the Rock my Savior* (89:26). Then Isaiah, in the midst of Israel's apostasy, knew that the Lord was *the Rock eternal* (Isaiah 26:4).

Reflection: *What experiences have you had in which God has proved himself to you as your Rock?*

A FORGIVING GOD

You were to Israel a forgiving God, though you punished their misdeeds.
(Psalm 99:8)

PARENTS KNOW THAT AT times their offspring need discipline as well as forgiveness. Israel, too, sometimes acted like a rebellious child needing God's discipline. God often allowed other nations to conquer them, but this discipline from God was within the context of his love. He was always ready to forgive and deliver them when they turned back to him.

The ultimate proof that God is a *forgiving God* was through the provision of his Son as the sacrifice for sin in which he took our punishment (1 John 4:10).

Knowing we have a *forgiving God* therefore gives us the confidence to own our sin and confess it to him. *If we confess our sins, he is faithful and just and will forgive us our sins and purify us from all unrighteousness* (1 John 1:9).

Reflection: *Forgetfulness is a human weakness so God doesn't forget our sins but "he remembers them no more" (Isaiah 43:25).*

THE MAKER OF HEAVEN AND EARTH

May you be blessed by the LORD, the Maker of heaven and earth,
(Psalm 115:15).

THE CONTEXT IN WHICH the Psalmist uses this title *"the Maker of Heaven and Earth"* is surprising for it does not occur, as we might expect, in passages in which God's creative handiwork is discussed. Rather, the title is attributed to God with reference to the way he blesses and helps his people.

The reference above occurs in a psalm connected to worship at the Passover Feast (115:15). Three references are from psalms probably sung by worshipers going to the Temple (121:2; 124:8; 134:3), and the last reference comes from a section of the Hallelujah Psalms sung at festivals (146:6).

In these Psalms the people affirmed the greatness of their Maker and expressed their devotion to him as the One who is worthy of their praise.

Reflection: *We too should worship and give thanks for "my help comes from the LORD, the Maker of heaven and earth" (Psalm 121:1–2).*

THE LORD IS YOUR SHADE

The LORD watches over you . . . the LORD is your shade at your right hand, (Psalm 121:5).

PSALM 121 IS A traveler's song highlighting the protection that the Lord provides for his people on their journey through life. Travelers ask, where could we get help when alone in hilly country (121:1)? Who is going to help if we lose our footing and fall (121:3)? What about the danger of long exposure to the sun (121:6)?

The danger of allowing ourselves to think like this, is that the unknown can paralyze us from taking the next step of faith in our journey. Rather, we need to make our preparations while acknowledging that our *help comes from the Lord* (121:2). We need to trust him to protect us and move on with our confidence in him.

Reflection: *Knowing the Lord as "your shade at your right hand", should give you the confidence you need so that you can say with the Psalmist, "the Lord will keep me from all harm" (121:7).*

THE HOLY ONE

Knowledge of the Holy One is Understanding (Proverbs 9:10)

IN THE OLD TESTAMENT, God is frequently spoken about as the *Holy One* and in the book of Proverbs the title *the Holy One* is associated with wisdom and knowledge (9:10; 30:3). Solomon wrote the first reference as advice to young men. It was written as a couplet, with two parallel statements about the *fear of the LORD* and the *knowledge of the Holy One*.

Knowledge and fear of God are therefore the basis for gaining wisdom and understanding. The *fear of the LORD* refers to a reverence for God in which we hold him in awe and avoid behaviors that bring dishonor to his name.

The *fear of the LORD* is presented as the key to *knowledge of the Holy One*, so as we learn to fear him so we seek to follow him.

Reflection: *Make it your aim to gain knowledge of the Holy One, growing in wisdom and understanding and a fear of the Lord.*

A STRONG TOWER

The name of the LORD is a strong tower;
The righteous run to it and are safe, (Proverbs 18:10).

TOWERS WERE OFTEN BUILT in vineyards so that watchmen could guard the vines, and occasionally they were seen in the countryside for protection of shepherds (2 Chronicles 26:10).

Strong towers were also built as part of the walls of fortified cities for Watchmen to keep guard. On one occasion about one thousand people took refuge in the tower at Shechem (Judges 9:49).

The *strong tower* was therefore a symbol of safety in time of trouble. These are the images that the writer of this proverb wanted his readers to have when he said, *the name of the Lord is a strong tower; the righteous run to it and are safe*. The name stands for the person and so the Lord himself provides protection for his people in times of difficulty.

Reflection: *As a "Strong Tower" the Lord provides a place of safety for us as we remain in him (John 15:4-7).*

THE MIGHTY ONE OF ISRAEL

(Isaiah 1:24)

THE TITLE THE MIGHTY One of Israel is used only once in the Bible, in a context in which Isaiah portrayed God as both the judge of the court, and the plaintiff who brought the charge against the nation of Israel. Heaven and earth were called to be witnesses (1:2) and the prophet conveyed the charge to the people. God was in covenant relationship with Israel, but they had turned away from him to worship idols (Isaiah 2:8).

The Lord Almighty is a name for God that emphasizes his omnipotent power. When it is linked to the title the *Mighty One of Israel,* the name indicates that his omnipotent power is intended as a blessing for his people.

History records however, that Israel ignored Isaiah's warning and that the Babylonian army eventually came and took them into captivity.

Reflection: *"My son, do not make light of the Lord's discipline, and do not lose heart when he rebukes you, because the Lord disciplines those he loves" (Hebrews 12:5-6).*

IMMANUEL—GOD WITH US
(Isaiah 8:7-8)

Usually we associate the name *Immanuel* with the birth of the Lord Jesus (Matthew 1:23), but the name was also used by Isaiah to give King Ahaz confidence that God was with his people. King Ahaz, however, was relying on his alliance with the King of Assyria.

Isaiah chapter 8 confirms an earlier prophecy about the demise of Israel and, instead of supporting King Ahaz, the Assyrian army would soon plunder the country. Shocked by his own prophetic words, Isaiah cried out in anguish *O Immanuel,* (8:8).

Isaiah chapter 8 contrasts the king and his people with Isaiah and his family who were a sign, sent by the Lord to the people to reinforce the message of Immanuel's presence. God was promising deliverance, assuring them of his love, and calling them to return to him, but if they refused they faced judgment.

Reflection: *We, like Israel, are often in danger of looking for security in the things of this world rather than in trusting our Lord.*

THE LIGHT OF ISRAEL . . . THE HOLY ONE, A FLAME
(Isaiah 10:17)

For God to be referred to as *the Light of Israel,* indicates that his presence was with his people, giving an understanding of himself and his ways. Israel was to *walk in the light of the Lord* by obeying him, (Isaiah 2:5).

The *Holy One* as *a flame* pictures God as a consuming fire. Israel was warned of the fire of God's punishment if they ever worshipped idols (Deuteronomy 4:24). But the fire of his punishment also came against the enemies of Israel.

Isaiah foretold such an event against Assyria, (10:17-19). *The king of Assyria had used the* pronouns "I" and "my" nine times, indicating his pride in what he had accomplished (Isaiah 10:13-14). Therefore the *Holy One* as a *flame* would destroy Assyria, an event that occurred with the fall of Nineveh in 612 BC.

Reflection: *The "Light of Israel" became in Christ the "light of the world" (John 8:12), so that we can live as "children of light" (Ephesians 5:8).*

NAMES FOR, AND REFERENCES TO, GOD THE FATHER

THE MIGHTY GOD

(Isaiah 10:21)

THE SOUTHERN KINGDOM OF Judah was taken captive by the Babylonians for their disobedience and idolatry, but Isaiah foretold that the day would come when a *remnant of Jacob (Israel) would return to the Mighty God* (10:21). This event took place following Judah's seventy years in exile beginning in 516 BC.

In the New Testament the name *the mighty God*, occurred when the Jewish council questioned Jesus, wanting to know whether or not he was the Christ (Luke 22:67–69).

Jesus replied, *From now on, the Son of Man will be seated at the right hand of the mighty God* (22:69). With these words Jesus looked beyond his crucifixion and resurrection, to his ascension in heaven with his Father. For Christians today these words speak of the Lord's triumph over death and his position of heavenly authority and power.

Reflection: *While the powers of darkness are pervasive and influence the nations, we need to remember that God has ultimate control of this world for he is "the Mighty God".*

THE LORD THE LORD—YAH, YHWH

The LORD, the LORD, is my strength and my song;
he has become my salvation, (Isaiah 12:2).

IN THE HEBREW LANGUAGE the names *the LORD the LORD* are "Yah" and "YHWH". The first name is a shortened form of the second name often used in the Psalms as a poetic form of the Lord's name.

The two names above give emphasis to his position as Israel's Lord and celebrates the greatness of his name. In the King James version of the Bible there is an instance where the Hebrew name Yah is retained by the translators, for we read . . . *extol him who rides upon the heavens by his name Yah, and rejoice before him* (Psalm 68:4).

We also have an example of the use of the name Yah in the word "Hallelujah" which occurs four times in Revelation 19. The word could be written "Hallelu—Yah" meaning "praise Yah" or "praise the LORD".

Reflection: *Celebrate today the greatness of our God who is "the LORD the LORD".*

A GLORIOUS CROWN, A SPIRIT OF JUSTICE, A SOURCE OF STRENGTH

(Isaiah 28:5–6)

SAMARIA WAS THE CAPITAL city of the northern kingdom and resplendent as a place of luxury and indulgence, *the pride of Ephraim's* (Israel's) *drunkards*. But Isaiah saw the glory of her crown as a *fading flower* (28:1, 4).

The invading Assyrians would soon destroy Samaria and therefore their state of spiritual decline should have been a warning to the rulers of Jerusalem in the south. But Jerusalem did not want to listen to Isaiah, for the sins of Samaria were also their sins.

Isaiah therefore looked beyond the impending invasions of Assyria and Babylon to a day when the nation would be restored.

- Then the *Lord Almighty will be a glorious crown* as ruler of the nation.
- He will be *a spirit of justice* to those in administration.
- To those who defend the gates of the city he will be their *source of strength*.

Reflection: *Remember, the Lord's discipline is aimed at restoring us to fellowship with himself.*

THE ROCK OF ISRAEL

(Isaiah 30:29)

GOD'S PEOPLE HAD BEEN rebellious and God was going to allow the Assyrians to bring to them *the bread of adversity and the water of affliction,* (30:20). However, the prophet envisaged a future day when the people would return to the Lord and play their instruments as they went up to the Temple, (30:29).

The Temple was positioned near the top of the hill, referred to as *the mountain of the Lord . . . the Rock of Israel.* This hill suggested solidarity, strength and permanence so these enduring qualities of the Temple Mount were also thought of as a symbol of God, *the Rock of Israel.* It was God alone who could bring stability to their lives and be a refuge for his people.

Reflection: *What a tragedy it was for Israel to ignore the fact that their Lord was "the Rock of Israel". We also need to remember that the Lord brings stability and security to our lives which should cause us to rejoice in him.*

THE HOLY ONE OF ISRAEL
(Isaiah 41:16b)

A REFERENCE TO HOLINESS included in a name for God indicates that he is separate from sin and devoted to his glory and honor. The name *the Holy One of Israel* therefore means that Israel was distinct among the nations in having a God who was holy.

Being the *Holy One of Israel,* God wanted to share the blessings of his holiness with Israel, so that he could show himself to the nations through the holiness of his people (Ezekiel 36:23). The prophet Isaiah used this name and the shortened form of the name, *the Holy One,* twenty-nine times. He was concerned to get the attention of his people.

As a nation they had lost their sense of God's holiness and needed to repent. They had *spurned the Holy One of Israel and turned their backs on him* (Isaiah 1:4).

Reflection: *The greatest blessing of holiness for us today is being able to live in relationship with the "Holy One" through our Savior Jesus Christ.*

THE GOD AND SAVIOR OF ISRAEL
(Isaiah 45:15)

GOD HAD REVEALED HIMSELF to the Hebrew people and established a covenant relationship with them as their God. In return for their obedience and worship, God would guide, protect and prosper the nation. He was a God that belonged exclusively to them and was both the *God and Savior of Israel.*

Israel, however, repeatedly broke God's laws and their impending judgment is foretold in Isaiah chapter 1, but in chapters 40 to 48, their return from exile in Babylon is also foretold.

As *God and Savior of Israel* he was to change the heart of Cyrus the Persian king, who would release Israel from their captivity in Babylon (45:1–5, 13). God had been hidden from them (45:15), but now had spoken openly (45:19) and so Isaiah foreshadowed a day when the invitation would go to all the nations, (45:22).

Reflection: *From the time of Christ the "God and Savior of Israel" has become the God and Savior of those from every nation.*

OUR REDEEMER

Our Redeemer–the Lord Almighty is his name, (Isaiah 47:4).

THE TITLE *REDEEMER* IS a title for God that occurs mostly in the Old Testament. In most instances Isaiah used the title to introduce a message from God and associated the name with one or more of his other names, e.g. 43:14.

Israel had a tightly knit society in which relatives usually cared for each other in time of need. A relative therefore might pay the redemption price for a person or his property if there was a debt, (Leviticus 25:25). The relative therefore acted as a "kinsman—redeemer" or Family Protector for a needy family member in trouble.

God was a "Kinsman—Redeemer" to his people. He had delivered them from slavery in Egypt, (Exodus 12:31) and Babylon (Isaiah 48:20). Then as their "Kinsman—Avenger" he punished those who afflicted Israel. The Babylonians were *never to rise again* (Isaiah 43:17).

Reflection: *It was God "our Redeemer" who so loved the world that he gave his only Son to redeem us (John 3:16).*

THE LORD YOUR MAKER

(Isaiah 51:12-13)

THE LORD YOUR MAKER is a title for God that was meant to reassure Israel of the special covenant relationship they had with him as their Lord.

Chapter 51 reminds Israel of how the Lord had cared for them in the past so they could have every confidence in his loving concern. In verses 12 and 13 we have the grandeur of God as creator of heaven and earth contrasted with Israel's enemies who are described as *mortal men who are but grass.*

Knowing the Lord as *your Maker* means they should experience joy and gladness along with his *comfort, compassion,* and salvation (51:3, 5). This response was not meant to be a passing emotion, but a permanent crown of *everlasting joy* (51:11).

Reflection: *Like the Israelites of old it is easy to forget "the Lord your Maker" by allowing the circumstances of life to cause you to fear. Rather, knowing him by this name brings an assurance of his love and protection which should cause you to rejoice.*

Names for, and References to, God the Father

THE GOD OF ALL THE EARTH
(Isaiah 54:5)

This title is only used by Isaiah. As Creator, God brought the earth into existence (Genesis 14:19) and through his Son sustains *all things by his powerful word* (Hebrews 1:3). Being *God of all the Earth* meant for Israel that he would act on their behalf.

Two examples of God's intervention are Israel's deliverance from slavery in Egypt and from their seventy years of exile in Babylon. It was this later release that Isaiah foreshadowed in chapter 54. Isaiah looked forward prophetically to a restored Israel when the *descendants will dispossess nations and settle in their desolate cities* (54:3).

This restoration would one day become a reality because of the promise made by Israel's *Maker . . . your husband . . . the Lord Almighty . . . the Holy One of Israel . . . your Redeemer . . .* who is *the God of all the earth* (54:5). Throughout his book Isaiah warned the people of God's impending judgment while calling them to repent.

Reflection: *God still wants to bless, but the obedience of God's people is a criterion for that blessing.*

THE POTTER
(Isaiah 64:8)

Both Isaiah and Jeremiah use the imagery of a potter and the clay. For Isaiah it was completely out of character for Israel, as the clay, to question God who created them. *Can the pot say to the potter, "He knows nothing"?* (Isaiah 29:16). *Does the pot say to the potter, "What are you making?"* (45:9).

These rhetorical questions by Israel indicate the rebellious attitude of the people and so Isaiah warned the nation, *"Woe to him who quarrels with his Maker"* (45:9).

Like Isaiah, Jeremiah also acknowledged the authority of the *Potter* over Israel as he watched a potter at work (Jeremiah 18:1–12). As the clay spun on the wheel, Jeremiah noticed that the pot became misshapen and so the potter started again and reshaped the clay *into another pot as seemed best to him* (Jeremiah 18:4).

Reflection: *Under the guiding hand of "the Potter" we can become "an instrument for noble purposes, made holy, useful to the Master and prepared to do any good work" (2 Timothy 2:21).*

THE SPRING OF LIVING WATER
(Jeremiah 2:13)

IN THE FARMING COMMUNITY of Jeremiah's day they dug small dams or cisterns into which the water could drain. These cisterns were usually lined with stone and plastered to make them water tight. A cracked or broken cistern meant that the water was lost and the animals would suffer. Jeremiah contrasted the Lord, *the spring of living water,* with the *broken cisterns that cannot hold water.*

The people were guilty of looking to political alliances with Egypt and Assyria for their protection. The prophet described these alliances as going to their rivers to drink (2:17–18). But the people had also *forsaken the spring of living water* through their worship of idols. The prophet estimated that they had *as many gods as they had towns* in Judah (2:28).

In chasing after support from Assyria and Egypt they had *dug their own cisterns, broken cisterns that cannot hold water.*

Reflection: *Pray for our nation that they will return to the Lord and drink from "the spring of living water".*

THE LIVING GOD
(Jeremiah 10:10)

THE TITLE THE LIVING God occurs twenty-eight times in Scripture and, as Jeremiah indicated, God is living and active in his creation.

- The Israelites heard the *living God* speak and saw his glory (Deuteronomy 5:24–26).
- Joshua affirmed the *living God* would drive out the inhabitants of Canaan (Joshua 3:10).
- David was surprised that a Philistine giant *should defy the armies of the living God* (1 Samuel 17:26).
- The heathen king Darius declared that everyone *must fear and reverence the God of Daniel. "For he is the living God"* (Daniel 6:26).
- Paul cried out to the crowd *to turn from these worthless things to the living God, who made heaven and earth and sea and everything in them* (Acts 14:15).

The *living God* has demonstrated his power both in creation and on behalf of his people.

Reflection: *What a privilege it is for us to be the "sons of the living God" (Romans 9:26), forming the "Church of the living God" (1 Timothy 3:15).*

THE ETERNAL KING
(Jeremiah 10:10)

IN JEREMIAH 10:1–16 THE prophet made a series of startling contrasts between the idols of the nations and the God of Israel. The Lord is declared to be the *true* and *living* God who rules forever with all authority as the *eternal King*.

As the *true and Living God* he had proved his faithfulness to Israel, demonstrated that his word could be trusted and brought reality to their lives and worship. In contrast the idols represented a false reality and were like *scarecrows in a melon patch* (10:5) capable only of scaring the birds.

As the *eternal King* the reign of the Lord is *from everlasting to everlasting* (Psalm 90:2). People everywhere are under his authority. As *eternal King* he is *King of the nations* (10:7) and *when their judgment comes they will perish* (10:15).

Reflection: *What a danger we face of allowing the artifacts of our culture to become our idols to replace "the eternal King" as our God. "Dear children, keep yourselves from idols" (1 John 5:21).*

THE LORD, THE GOD OF ISRAEL
(Jeremiah 11:2-3)

THE LORD, THE GOD *of Israel* is a title that highlights the exclusive covenant relationship that existed between the LORD and Israel. A summary statement of this covenant appears in the words, *"you will be my people, and I will be your God."* (Jeremiah 11:4b; 24:7).

The people in Jeremiah's day had broken the terms of this covenant relationship and nearly fifty times Jeremiah prefaced his messages with this title, or one of its variations such as, *The LORD Almighty the God of Israel says . . .* or, *The LORD the Holy One of Israel says . . .*

The southern kingdom of Judah was later exiled to Babylon, but because of his covenant, the Lord would later bring them back from exile. Thus the LORD the God of Israel says *I will give them a heart to know me that I am the LORD* (24:5–7).

Reflection: *We too are "heirs together with Israel, members together in one body and sharers together in the promise in Christ Jesus, (Ephesians 3:6).*

THE HOPE OF ISRAEL
(Jeremiah 14:8)

JEREMIAH REFERRED TO GOD as the *Hope of Israel* because he was confident that God would be faithful to the covenant he had made with his people (Jeremiah 14:21). Therefore he could approach God with an expectation that he would hear his prayer, for God was the *Hope of Israel, their Savior.*

Israel had sinned and failed to keep God's laws but in making his appeal to God, Jeremiah identified with the sins of the people when he said, *our sins testify against us, . . . our backsliding is great;* and *we have sinned against you* (14:7).

Jeremiah was concerned for the honor of the name of the Lord (14:7, 21) and continued to plead the nation's cause, (14:19–22).

Reflection: *We must identify the sins of our nation as our sins and seek the Lord in prayer for their forgiveness. Like Jeremiah, we need to be concerned for the honor of the name of the Lord and call on him as the only hope for our nation.*

THE ARM OF THE LORD
(Isaiah 51:9)

O ARM OF THE LORD awake; is a metaphor in which the Lord's strength is personified and he is called on to "awake" and show his power on Israel's behalf. But the Lord was not "asleep". Rather, it was Israel who needed to be reminded of how the Lord had delivered them in the past, (51:6).

What was the problem? Why had Isaiah assumed the Lord was "sleeping"? The Lord addressed the problem when he said, *you forget the LORD your Maker* (51:13). Then he continued, *Awake, awake! Rise up, O Jerusalem* (51:17).

In the verses that follow the Lord explained why Israel had to endure the rebuke of their God through the torment of their enemies.

Reflection: *Sin in our lives will always grieve the Holy Spirit and quench his activity. The lesson we can learn from Israel is that when people repent and return to the Lord, they find that "the arm of the Lord is not too short to save" (Isaiah 59:1).*

THE LORD OUR RIGHTEOUSNESS—YHWH TSIDKENU
(Jeremiah 23:6)

DURING JEREMIAH'S TIME, MEN had been forced to build King Jehoiakim's palace without pay so Jeremiah warned the king, *Woe to him who builds his palace by unrighteousness* (22:13).

The Lord had showed his righteousness in the law, but the leaders and people of Judah also failed to live righteously and so Jeremiah warned that they would be taken into captivity by the Babylonians. Jeremiah also wrote prophetically about the future coming of Messiah who *will reign wisely and do what is just and right in the land.*

In his days Judah will be saved and Israel will live in safety. This is the name by which he will be called: The LORD Our Righteousness, (Jeremiah 23:5, 6).

Reflection: *How can a righteous God forgive our sins? Paul tells us that we can be in a right relationship with God because, "God made him, (the Lord Jesus), who had no sin to be sin for us, so that in him we might become the righteousness of God" (2 Corinthians 5:21).*

THE ONE I PRAISE
(Jeremiah 17:14)

IN THIS VERSE THE word for praise, "tehilla", that Jeremiah used to exalt the Lord is also used elsewhere to proclaim the excellence and renown of the Lord in the midst of adverse circumstances, e.g. Psalm 22:3.

With such a great God, Jeremiah felt confident to request healing and deliverance, *for you are the One I Praise* (17:14).

Jeremiah stands as a shining example of someone who endured cruel persecution and yet retained his confidence in God. His unsympathetic listeners were a people who had forsaken God. Jeremiah knew that *the man who trusts in the Lord is like a tree planted by the water . . . that does not fear the heat* or *drought* but remains *green* and never *fails to bear fruit* (17:7–8).

Reflection: *When we learn to praise the Lord we find our strength to face difficult situations, for we are like a tree planted beside the river, unaffected by the drought. Make it your aim to live for his "renown and praise and honor" (Jeremiah 13:11).*

THE LORD IS THERE—YHWH SHAMMAH
(Ezekiel 48:35)

EZEKIEL WAS IN CAPTIVITY along with about ten thousand people from Judah, eleven years before the Babylonians finally destroyed Jerusalem and its Temple in 586 BC.

Following the downfall, Ezekiel's message (chapters 33–48) changed to one of comfort, (36:27). The people are pictured as a valley of dry bones with God restoring them to life and returning them to the land of Israel (chapter 37). God had been disciplining his people in Babylon so that his holiness might be seen through them (36:23).

Just as Ezekiel had earlier seen a vision of the glory of the Lord departing from the temple, he now saw the Lord's glory returning (43:4). *This is where I will live among the Israelites forever* (43:7). Ezekiel's book ends with the final confirming statement of the Lord's name on the city, *The LORD Is There*.

Reflection: *God is still in covenant relationship with his people, so wherever his people are and whatever the circumstances: The LORD Is There.*

THE KING OF HEAVEN
(Daniel 4:37)

NEBUCHADNEZZAR, THE KING OF Babylon had a seven year period of insanity, but when sanity returned he accepted that Daniel's God was the *King of heaven*, (4:37).

But the *King of Heaven* also extended his kingdom to earth as John the Baptist announced, *Repent, for the kingdom of heaven is near* (Matthew 3:2)—words that were also repeated by Jesus (Matthew 4:17).

There are thirty-one references to the *kingdom of heaven* in the book of Matthew explaining what his kingdom is like and who may enter it. The *King of heaven* therefore continues to establish his kingdom on earth through his rule in the lives of his people.

Reflection: *The Lord's Prayer makes it clear that his kingdom has come wherever God's will is done "on earth as it is in heaven" (Matthew 6:10). However, his kingdom will not be complete until the "kingdom of the world has become the kingdom of our Lord and of his Christ, and he will reign for ever and ever" (Revelation 11:15).*

THE ANCIENT OF DAYS
(Daniel 7:13)

The *Ancient of Days* is a title of honor that emphasizes God's wisdom and his enduring preeminence. The title occurs three times in Daniel chapter 7 where the grandeur and authority of the *Ancient of Days* is presented (7:9–10).

With him is the *Son of Man,* (7:13), a title that was claimed by the Lord Jesus (Matthew 24:30). There are also present many thousands of people from every nation and language on earth, who bring their worship to him (Daniel 7:14).

This is a scene of great glory and authority in which the *Ancient of Days* demonstrates his ultimate control over the world. The nations of the world are also contrasted with the *Son of Man,* who is given *authority, glory and sovereign power,* along with everlasting dominion over a kingdom that will never pass away or be destroyed (7:14).

Reflection: *Do you fear the future or look forward with confidence knowing that the "Ancient of Days" and the "Son of Man" have future events in their control?*

PRINCE OF PRINCES, THE PRINCE OF THE HOST
(Daniel 8:11, 25)

Both of these titles for God occur in a context in which the prophet Daniel foreshadowed the coming of an evil ruler who would dominate Israel and destroy their worship.

The prophecy was fulfilled towards the end of the second century B.C. when a Greek king called Antiochus Epiphanes (the Magnificent) led his army against Israel. You can read of the evil exploits of Antiochus in 1 Maccabees 1. For Daniel however, God was *the Prince of the host* (8:11), and the *Prince of Princes* (8:25).

The term *Prince* means ruler or commander, so Daniel acknowledged God as the ruler over Israel, as well as ruler of the world. For a time Antiochus seemed unstoppable, but Daniel's brief note mentions his demise, (8:25). Antiochus is thought to have died in 164 B.C.

Reflection: *Evil rulers can dominate but their fall is certain for the "Prince of the host", the "Prince of princes" is the LORD who "will not give his glory to another" (Isaiah 42:8).*

THE WATCHMAN OVER EPHRAIM
(Hosea 9:8)

EPHRAIM WAS JOSEPH'S YOUNGER son whose descendants became a tribe of Israel with their territory in Canaan also known as Ephraim (Joshua 17:15). Eventually they became the leading tribe of the northern kingdom of Israel.

Watchmen over ancient cities were positioned on the towers of a city wall to alert the people if an enemy or messenger was approaching. Therefore, as a spiritual watchman, Hosea spoke God's message to the people as a *watchman over Ephraim.*

However, Hosea was absolutely confident that he was not acting alone as a prophet, for he could say *the prophet, along with my God, is the watchman over Ephraim,* (Hosea 9:8).

Reflection: *To know that the Lord is a watchman over us should be a source of great comfort, for we know that he acts in our best interests. "He is able to keep you from falling" (Jude 24) while also "disciplining us for our good, that we may share in his holiness" (Hebrews 12:10).*

MY HUSBAND
(Hosea 2:16, 19, 20)

THE HUSBAND/WIFE RELATIONSHIP OF love and faithfulness which should characterize a marriage is presented in Hosea as a metaphor of the relationship between Israel and their Lord, (2:16). Other prophets such as Isaiah (54:5) and Jeremiah (3:14) also refer to the Lord as the *husband* of Israel.

For Hosea, Israel's relationship with God was one of spiritual adultery. The prophet records his disastrous marriage in which his unfaithful wife was sent away. Later she was restored as his wife (Hosea 3:1–2). The Lord used Hosea's marriage to remind Israel of their broken relationship with him, in which he looked forward to the day when they would return to him. Then God would be their *husband* in a marriage characterized by faithfulness.

We too face the problem of spiritual adultery in worshipping the gods of our culture. These gods may include anything that we regard as more important than God.

Reflection: *To think of the Lord as "my Husband", should lead to a life spent in devotion to him.*

THE PRIDE OF JACOB
(Amos 8:7)

GOD LOVED HIS PEOPLE Israel who were to him, *The Pride of Jacob,* (Psalm 47:4). But in Amos 8:7, the term is used as a synonym for God and highlights the privilege Jacob/Israel felt in owning the LORD as their God.

Abraham, Isaac and Jacob were the three generations of the family that God chose for himself to start the nation of Israel. But Israel was to go into spiritual decline and injustice was common in the time of Amos. The poor people were mistreated, the scales in the market place were falsified and prices were inflated (Amos 8:5).

Against this background, Amos said *The LORD has sworn by the Pride of Jacob: "I will never forget anything they have done".* With these words God took an oath by his name *the Pride of Jacob* to judge his disobedient people.

Reflection: *It is amazing to think that in spite of our failings, God has loved us and from the beginning chosen us to salvation (2 Thessalonians 2:13).*

THE LORD YOUR GOD
(Amos 9:15)

IN AMOS CHAPTER 9:11–15 there is a message of hope that *the LORD your God* would restore *David's fallen tent* (9:11), and restore Israel to their land (9:14–15). King David's "tent" was the place of worship in Jerusalem and was associated with celebration and the playing of instruments, (1 Chronicles 16:4–6). At this time, the sacrifices associated with the Tabernacle of Moses continued to be offered at Gibeon (1 Chronicles 21:29).

When the prophecy by Amos was fulfilled around 300 years later, ending Judah's captivity in Babylon, it was Nehemiah who looked to the pattern of worship that had been modeled by King David (Nehemiah 12:24).

Later the Apostle James reminded the Jerusalem Council of the words of Amos (Acts 15:16). The Jewish people, along with the worship and celebration associated with *David's tent,* were now restored to the Church.

Reflection: *The "LORD your God" fulfilled his promise. As a Church we are "all one in Christ Jesus" in worshipping the Lord (Galatians 3:28).*

THE ONE WHO BREAKS OPEN THE WAY
(Micah 2:13)

EVEN THOUGH MICAH LIVED during a time of Judah's spiritual and social decline he saw that God would forgive the nation their sins. He used the imagery of the nation as sheep in a sheepfold (2:12). While a sheepfold gives protection to the sheep overnight, it becomes a prison if there is no shepherd to release them the next day.

Thus Micah presented a picture of the Lord as the *One who breaks open the way*, for he will break down the gate and release the imprisoned sheep. Then as their true Shepherd he will go before them and once again his people will follow him (2:13).

This vivid picture was fulfilled in the return of Israel from their Babylonian captivity, and later in the coming of Messiah. It was Micah who saw Bethlehem as the place of Messiah's birth (5:2).

Reflection: *The Lord Jesus continues to be our Shepherd, "the One who breaks open the way" and sets people free from their sin.*

THE LORD OUR GOD
(Micah 4:5)

SEVERAL TIMES IN THE Old Testament the prophets combined the two names "Lord" and "God" using pronouns such as "our", "your", "their" or "his". In doing this, they often compared the gods of the nations with their God.

Micah used this combined name in chapter 5:4, where he saw the glory of Messiah linked to the *name of the Lord his God*. He also imagined a conversation in which the enemies confess that they had questioned the presence of the *LORD your God* (7:10), as they turn in fear to *the LORD our God* (7:16–17).

Coming judgment was a burden to Micah, but he also saw that the Lord would one day forgive his people. *Who is a God like you who pardons sins and forgives* (7:18–20).

Reflection: *The world today follows many gods of which wealth sport and pleasure are just a sample. Let us today affirm the words of Micah, "We will walk in the name of the LORD our God for ever and ever" (4:5).*

A REFUGE

(Nahum 1:7)

NAHUM VIVIDLY DESCRIBES THE plunder of the Assyrian army who destroyed the cities of Israel and took the people captive, (Nahum 3:3). The thought that the Assyrians would return and deal with Judah in a similar manner must have filled the people with fear.

But God wanted his people to trust him and not to be afraid, for *the Lord is good, a refuge in times of trouble*. To refer to the Lord as *a refuge* highlights his presence among his people as a stronghold against attack.

It was a reassuring message for Nahum to prophesy that God would judge Nineveh, the capital of Assyria, and that their army would not return to destroy Judah (Nahum 1:14–15).

Reflection: *The prophet Jonah had once warned Nineveh of its wickedness and they had turned to God in repentance (Jonah 3:6-10). Now they had forgotten God and were about to be destroyed. Pray that our nation will not turn away from God but will find him as "a refuge".*

A WALL OF FIRE

(Zechariah 2:5)

ZECHARIAH WAS BORN DURING the time of Israel's captivity in Babylon and had returned to Jerusalem to find it in ruins. As both a prophet and priest he led the people in worship and helped in rebuilding the temple (4:8).

Zechariah in his vision saw a day when Jerusalem would be a *city without walls because of the great number of men and livestock in it* (2:4). The Lord then gave this wonderful promise to his people. *I will be a wall of fire around it . . . and I will be its glory within* (2:5).

Ancient cities sought protection from their enemies behind their stone walls, but Jerusalem had no need of a city wall, for the presence of the Lord as *"its glory"* would give his people protection as they were *the apple of his eye* (2:8).

Reflection: *The picture of the Lord as a "wall of fire" and his people as the "apple of his eye" are vivid images of the Lord's protecting presence and his love.*

A REFINER AND PURIFIER
(Malachi 3:3)

FROM ANCIENT TIMES THE smelting of iron and other metals in kilns using intense heat has allowed men to remove the impurities from these metals.

So the prophet Malachi likened the Lord to a *refiner and purifier of silver,* which is another way of saying that God was concerned to ensure that those who serve him should be a holy people.

What is important is the principle that when the *refiner and purifier* judges his people, it is with a view to dealing with their sin and restoring them to himself. Often it is through trials and difficulties that God seeks to develop our character, but we too are to *purify ourselves from everything that contaminates body and spirit* (2 Corinthians 7:1).

Reflection: *No one likes the heat of the furnace, but his purpose is that our faith . . . "though refined by fire may be proved genuine and may result in praise, glory and honor when Jesus Christ is revealed" (1 Peter 1:7).*

MY FATHER
(Luke 2:49)

IN THE OLD TESTAMENT the term "Father" is only used for God in relation to the nation of Israel, for they referred to themselves as the *Children of Abraham,* and to Abraham as their father.

No name for God better illustrates the difference between the Old and New Testaments, for in the New Testament Jesus frequently used the title *My Father,* in speaking of his Heavenly Father, and the title *Your Father,* when speaking to his followers.

By the time Jesus was twelve years old he understood who his heavenly Father was, for he referred to the Temple as *my Father's House* (Luke 2:48–49). The next verse indicates that his parents did not understand what he was saying, because no one to this point in time had ever referred to God in such a personal way by calling him Father.

Reflection: *Knowing God as your Father means that he cares for you as part of his family. As his child you should be a responsible family member.*

THE LORD OF THE HARVEST
(Matthew 9:38)

PALESTINE WAS MOSTLY SUITED to pastoral farming, but in Galilee the land was also tilled for crops and fruit trees.

Against this rural background Jesus *saw the crowds . . . like sheep without a shepherd* (Matthew 9:36). He then spoke to his disciples about the size of the harvest, the need for more workers and the need to pray that the *Lord of the harvest* would *send out workers into his harvest field.*

In this metaphor as the *Lord of the harvest,* the Father is portrayed as a farmer who needs workers to help him gather in the harvest. Without laborers the harvest will have to wait for other harvesters. It is interesting to note that following this teaching about the harvest, the twelve disciples (Matthew 10) and seventy-two disciples (Luke 10:1–12) were sent out.

Reflection: *Think of yourself as a worker in the midst of a plentiful harvest. Pray for the compassion and desire to do this work and pray that more workers will join you.*

THE LIVING FATHER
(John 6:57)

JESUS USED THE TITLE the *Living Father* when he taught about himself as *the bread of life* (John 6:57, 58). Then he reminded his listeners how God fed the Israelites with manna in the desert (Numbers 11:7–9).

This *bread from heaven* was God's provision and now the *Living Father* had again provided *the bread of God . . . who gives life to the world* (John 6:33). Jesus explained that *the one who feeds on me will live because of me* (6:51).

The idea of feeding on him had its roots in the Old Testament "peace" or "fellowship" offering. In making their offering the worshipers were given a portion of the offering back so that they could eat it with their friends. The offering therefore signified both peace with God and fellowship with others.

Reflection: *When we feed on Christ at Communion, we are reminded that we have peace with God through our Lord Jesus Christ (Romans 5:1) and that we enjoy fellowship with one another (1 John 1:7).*

THE JUDGE
(Psalm 96:10)

THE BIBLE INDICATES THAT both God the Father and the Lord Jesus are mentioned in their role as *Judge*. When the Old Testament speaks of God as judge, he is viewed as both sovereign ruler and adjudicator. The Psalmist noted this dual role when he said, *"The Lord reigns . . . He will judge the people with equity"* (Psalm 96:10).

In the New Testament God has delegated this authority to his Son. *The Father judges no one, but has entrusted all judgment to the Son* (John 5:22).

Today salvation is offered to all who will confess that Jesus is Lord (Romans 10:9). But there is a time of judgment coming when we must all *give an account to him who is ready to judge the living and the dead* (1 Peter 4:5).

Reflection: *Judgment for sinners will mean eternal separation from God (Matthew 13:49). For God's people however, judgment refers to an evaluation, when our lives and service for the Lord will be assessed and we will either gain or lose our reward (1 Corinthians 3:12-15).*

ABBA FATHER
(Mark 14:36)

THE TITLES *ABBA* AND *Father* occur together three times in the New Testament, (Mark 14:36; Romans 8:15: Galatians 4:6). This Aramaic name indicates an intimate, loving and respectful relationship between children and their Father. *Abba* was an expression used only by family members and slaves were forbidden to use it.

Mark 14:36 is from a scene in the garden of Gethsemane where Jesus knew his trial and crucifixion were approaching and in prayer he addressed his heavenly Father, using the family name of *Abba Father*.

He then requested that if possible the "cup" be taken from him. The symbolism of the cup referred to both his joy in doing his Father's will, and the suffering that he would experience at the trial and on the cross as he bore the wrath of God against sin.

Reflection: *Through Christ we too can come to the Father (John 14:6), and as a family member know God as our "Abba Father". The intimacy of our family relationship assures us of his love, care and protection.*

Names for, and References to, God the Father

THE IMMORTAL GOD
(Romans 1:20–23)

IN THESE VERSES PAUL presents a picture of the *eternal power, the divine nature* and the glory of the *Immortal God* in contrast to the worship of idols by the pagan world. To be *mortal* is to face the aging process leading to death, but the existence of the *Immortal God* is described as *glorious*, for he is untouched by death and decay.

The context of the above verses is a discussion on the *wrath of God* that *is being revealed from heaven* against people who *suppress the truth* about him, (1:18).

Then Paul outlines the depravity of mind that occurs when people choose other gods (1:24–32), and are subject to God's wrath in this life and the next.

Reflection: *What a future we look forward to "Our Savior, Christ Jesus, has destroyed death and has brought life and immortality to light through the gospel" (2 Timothy 1:10). Immortality has been assured to those who know Christ as their Savior and who worship the "Immortal God".*

THE GOD OF THE JEWS . . . THE GOD OF THE GENTILES
(Romans 3:29)

IN THIS VERSE PAUL asked the questions, *Is God the God of the Jews only? Is he not the God of Gentiles too?* His answer to the second question is clearly "Yes", for there is *only one God,* who justifies people on the basis of faith (3:29), from whatever background.

The term "justify" indicated that God had declared the people of faith as righteous. *Abraham believed God and it was credited to him as righteousness* (4:3), so it is through faith also that the righteousness of Christ is credited to us (4:23–24).

Today people are divided by social, cultural, economic, and religious differences, but since the gospel was *to the Jew first,* (Rom.1:16), *God* has *grafted* Gentile believers into the *olive tree* of Jewish believers. (Romans 11:17).

Reflection: *The Church gives expression to this unity of believers, "His purpose was to create in himself one new man out of the two, thus making peace" (Ephesians 2:15).*

THE GOD OF HOPE
(Romans 15:13)

PAUL USES THE WORD "hope" not as an uncertain wish, but as an assurance of a future reality. This "hope" should lead us to an increased confidence in God in regard to our present circumstances. Paul explained that to know him as the *God of hope* would mean that we can enjoy in this life some of the blessings of the life to come.

The words "fill" and "overflow" in the above verse indicate that there is a lavish supply of *joy and peace* for us to experience from the *God of hope*.

To trust in the *God of hope* means that our future is secure in him and that we have his blessings to enjoy. The alternative is to be *without hope and without God in the world,* (Ephesians 2:12).

Reflection: *Not to know the "God of hope" is to live a life that is hopeless. Meditate on the blessings that you have experienced through having your hope in him and give him thanks.*

THE ONLY WISE GOD
(Romans 16:27)

THROUGHOUT THE AGES PEOPLE have sought for the meaning of life through philosophies and religious practices, but Paul declared that such wisdom was foolishness (1 Corinthians 3:19).

We read that *the fear of the LORD is the beginning of wisdom* (Proverbs 9:10) and a knowledge of God and his wisdom is revealed through the gospel as the Father draws people to Christ (John 6:44). Therefore, the Lord God alone is the source of true wisdom for he is *the only wise God*.

It is important for us to understand that it is *through the Church the manifold wisdom of God should be made known to the rulers and authorities in the heavenly realms,* (Ephesians 3:10). As Paul contemplated the wisdom of God in worship he says, *To the only wise God be glory forever through Jesus Christ! Amen* (Romans 16:27).

Reflection: *What a privilege to be invited by "the only wise God" to ask for wisdom, knowing that he "gives generously to all without finding fault" (James 1:5).*

THE FATHER OF COMPASSION
(2 Corinthians 1:3)

PAGAN WORSHIPPERS VIEWED THEIR gods as incapable of feeling, thinking that it was impossible for a god to be influenced by the needs of a human being. Further, they believed that feeling compassion for someone less fortunate was a sign of weakness.

In contrast to this outlook, the Lord revealed himself to Israel as their God who would take pity on them. David could say, *as a father has compassion on his children, so the LORD has compassion on those who fear him* (Psalm 103:13).

When Jesus was on earth he shared the compassionate nature of his Father. Eight times in the Gospels we read that Jesus had compassion on people and on each occasion he performed a miracle to heal or to help them. His example and teaching involved a radical change in lifestyle that would one day change attitudes around the world.

Reflection: *How do you respond to the needs of others? Pray that the "Father of compassion" will make you a more compassionate person.*

THE GOD OF ALL COMFORT
(2 Corinthians 1:3b-4)

FOR GOD TO BE referred to as *the God of all comfort* means that he is the source of our encouragement and strength. Paul therefore urged the Christians at Corinth to also provide encouragement and support to others in need. God wants to show that he is the *God of all comfort* through us his people.

Paul's teaching about the Lord being the *God of all comfort,* is against a background of the Lord's suffering. As Christ suffered we too can expect to suffer, for the world that rejected Christ will also reject us. Paul made this clear when he said that *just as you share in our sufferings, so also you share in our comfort* (1:7).

Reflection: *"To this you were called, because Christ suffered for you, leaving you an example, that you should follow in his steps" (1 Peter 2:21). Use your experience of suffering to bring comfort to others that they too may know the Lord as "the God of all comfort".*

THE GOD OF LOVE
(2 Corinthians 13:11)

GOD SHOWS HIMSELF TO be the *God of love* in the way he saves and blesses his people, but his love is always in the context of his holiness and his discipline, (Leviticus 10:1–3).

Because Israel failed to obey God, they spent forty years wandering in the wilderness when they could have proceeded to enter Canaan, and avoided their punishment. (Deuteronomy 2:14).

The only permanent solution for sin was for the *God of love* to come to earth in the person of his Son and to die for the sin of the world. The coming of Christ and his death for us is the evidence that there is a *God of love*.

Reflection: *God's purpose in loving us is to develop in us his character of love and holiness. As the "God of Love", he disciplines us for our good that we may share his holiness" (Hebrews 12:10). Thus we are able "to love one another" (1 John 4:11).*

GOD OUR FATHER
(Ephesians 1:2)

THE TITLE GOD OUR *Father* occurs in nine of Paul's New Testament letters as an opening greeting and affirmation of who God is.

In the New Testament, the name *Father* indicates a family relationship, and knowing God as *our Father* links God's people together as spiritual brothers and sisters in his family. Ephesians 1:2 connects *grace and peace* with *God our Father and the Lord Jesus Christ*. God's *grace* is always described as an undeserved gift. It is God's response to our helplessness.

In extending his *grace* to us we therefore become the recipients of his *peace*. To have this *peace* means that we are restored to a relationship with God in which we are no longer under his wrath. Thus we have *peace with God through our Lord Jesus Christ* (Romans 5:1).

Reflection: *The qualities of grace and peace from "God our Father" provide a basis for living in God's family. Being at peace with God allows us to share his grace with others.*

THE GLORIOUS FATHER
(Ephesians 1:17)

To speak about God as the *glorious Father* is to acknowledge that glory is a characteristic of his being. The Bible helps us to understand the nature of his glory in the following descriptive texts:

- He has a *glorious and awesome name,* (Deuteronomy 28:58), and we should *praise his glorious name* (1 Chronicles 29:13).
- People are to speak of the *glorious splendor of your majesty* (Psalm 145:5).
- He has a *glorious presence* (Isaiah 3:8).
- *Glorious and majestic are his deeds* (Psalm 111:3).
- In times of battle he was a *glorious sword* to Israel (Deuteronomy 33:29).
- It is from his *glorious riches* that we are *strengthened with power through his Spirit* (Ephesians 3:16).

Reflection: *It is the glorious Father who sent the Spirit of wisdom and revelation to his people so that we may know him better (Ephesians 1:17). Knowing him better should be our aim, for one day we will be presented before his "glorious presence" (Jude 24).*

TO HIM WHO IS ABLE
(Ephesians 3:20)

In Ephesians 3 Paul wanted to stretch the thinking of his readers as he spoke of God as the one *who is able to do immeasurably more than all we ask or imagine,* (3:20).

So knowing that God *is able,* requires us to think beyond the usual scope of our limited imagination to new possibilities in the way we pray.

Knowing God as the One, *who is able,* is to experience his power at work in us, making things that are beyond our imagination a reality. We therefore must be careful not to limit God by our lack of imagination and our failure to pray and ask.

Reflection: *Paul's statement about "him who is able" should come to us as a wake-up call to allow God to stretch our thinking as to what is possible. God wants you to know him, and maybe he wants you to experience his power in your life in fresh and different ways. Why don't you give him the invitation?*

THE GOD OF PEACE
(Philippians 4:9)

PAUL ENCOURAGED THE PHILIPPIANS to rejoice and not to be anxious, for through their prayers they should know *the peace of God* guarding their hearts and minds, (Philippians 4:7). Further they were told they needed to monitor their thought life and think about things that were pure with a mind-set that supported a wholesome lifestyle.

So we too need to live this way, for Paul assures us that *the God of Peace* will be with us, (Philippians 4:4–9).

The *God of Peace* was also instrumental in raising the Lord Jesus from the dead, so with Satan's power broken, *the God of Peace* is able to work in us so that we live our lives to please him (Hebrews 13:20–21). Further, the *God of Peace* is also said to *sanctify* us by setting us apart for himself as his holy people (Colossians 1:20).

Reflection: *Holiness should characterize the way we live our lives. How has "the God of Peace" made a difference to your lifestyle?*

THE KING ETERNAL, IMMORTAL, INVISIBLE, THE ONLY GOD
(1 Timothy 1:17)

PAUL WROTE TO TIMOTHY and reflected on the miracle of what God had done for him in Christ which caused him in turn to worship, acknowledging God as *the King eternal, immortal, invisible, the only God.*

As the *King eternal*, God has absolute authority. Such is the enduring nature of his reign that David acknowledged that his *kingdom is an everlasting kingdom, and* his *dominion endures through all generations* (Psalm 145:13).

But as the *King eternal* he is also *immortal, invisible, the only God*. Whereas his eternity refers to his timeless existence, his immortality indicates that he is untouched by death and decay that affects creation. As Paul explains, God *alone is immortal who lives in unapproachable light* (1 Timothy 6:16).

Reflection: *As we contemplate the grandeur of "the King eternal, immortal, invisible, the only God", like Paul we should acknowledge him in our worship as deserving of all honor and glory. "To him belongs eternal praise" (Psalm 111:10).*

Names for, and References to, God the Father

THE SAVIOR OF ALL MEN
(1 Timothy 4:9, 10)

PAUL IN HIS PASTORAL letters to Timothy and Titus lists five "trustworthy sayings" in connection with the names of God the Father and the Lord Jesus. Paul's claim that these statements are "trustworthy" is evidence of his confidence in God's word.

This is a trustworthy saying—

- *we have put our hope in the living God who is the Savior of all men* (1 Timothy 4:9, 10).
- *Christ Jesus came into the world to save sinners* (1 Timothy 1:15).
- *if we died with him, we will also live with him; if we endure we will also reign with him* (2 Timothy 2:11, 12).
- *having been justified by his grace, we might become heirs having the hope of eternal life.* (Titus 3:7, 8).
- *if anyone sets his heart on being an overseer, he desires a noble task* (1 Timothy 3:1).

Reflection: *"God the Savior of all men" can be trusted. How do these trustworthy statements above affect your confidence to trust God and his word?*

GOD, THE BLESSED AND ONLY RULER
(1 Timothy 6:15, 16)

RULERS GOVERN OR JUDGE and in the Bible both God the Father and the Lord Jesus are given this title. The word has the idea of being first in order by rank and so God has this position and authority.

As *the blessed and only Ruler*, these verses speak of him as *King of kings and Lord of lords*, having *immortality* and being the source of all life.

There is reference to him also being unseen and dwelling in *unapproachable light* which may be a reference to God's revelation of his glory to Moses (Exodus 33:22; 16:10). The scene therefore highlights the supreme and absolute authority of God as ruler over all.

Reflection: *It is when we submit to the authority of God and acknowledge him as the "Blessed and only Ruler", we start to understand that he acts in our best interests. Then we appreciate his many blessings. Learn to "Submit yourselves then to God" (James 4:7), "the Blessed and only Ruler".*

KING OF Kings AND LORD OF Lords
(1 Timothy 6:15)

THE LORD JESUS HAS promised to return and establish his Kingdom. This great occasion will be at the direction of God and be the ultimate proof that he is King over all kings and Lord over all lords, the *ruler of the kings of the earth* (Revelation 1:5).

Heaven and earth is the realm of God's kingdom, but he also has a spiritual kingdom in the lives of his people. Jesus taught that to enter the kingdom *you must be born again* (John 3:7).

In his ministry of healing and deliverance Jesus also demonstrated that his kingdom had come (Matthew 12:28), but there is a future kingdom which we look forward to as "heirs" of his kingdom, (James 2:5).

Reflection: *On that future day, the glory of his kingdom will be seen by all when he establishes his authority over a new heaven and a new earth (Revelation 21:1). Then all will know that he is "King of kings and Lord of lords".*

THE MAJESTY IN HEAVEN
(Hebrews 1:3)

TWICE IN THE BOOK of Hebrews God the Father is referred to as *the Majesty in heaven* (1:3; 8:1). The title emphasizes his supreme greatness, his position of absolute authority and the splendor of his being.

Both verses refer to the Lord Jesus, as seated in the place of honor given to the Son at the right hand of the Majesty. It also expresses the acceptance by the Father of the Son's work in reconciling men and women to him.

The title of *Majesty* was often used by the Psalmist to speak of the splendor and majesty of the Lord's appearance (1 Chronicles 16:27; Psalm 45:3; 110:3). In contrast, Isaiah states that men will hide from the *splendor of his majesty*, for the Day of the LORD will be a day of judgment (2:10, 19, 21).

Reflection: *Meeting "the Majesty of heaven" will either be a cause of fear, or rejoicing. For God's people, it will be a day when we will worship as never before.*

THE FATHER OF SPIRITS
(Hebrews 12:9)

No one likes to be disciplined, but the writer of Hebrews argued that just as fathers discipline their children, so it is necessary for God as the *Father of spirits* to discipline his children. A good father uses discipline wisely, but a father who does not use discipline treats his children as *illegitimate* (12:8).

Unlike the Roman father, who was sometimes capricious in the exercise of physical discipline, *the Father of spirits* watches over our spirits so that our thought life, which includes our attitudes and motivations, are under his scrutiny.

Therefore we grieve the Spirit of God, not only by our sinful actions, but also when we fail to guard our thinking or adopt attitudes that are not in keeping with the *mind of Christ,* (1 Corinthians 2:16).

Reflection: *God is holy and when we fail to live a holy life we invite discipline from the "Father of spirits". "God disciplines us for our good that we may share in his holiness" (Hebrews 12:10).*

A CONSUMING FIRE
(Hebrews 12:28–29)

This metaphor of God as *a consuming fire* is quoted by the writer from Deuteronomy 4:24. The children of Israel were warned not to forget God's covenant and not to make idols or to worship them, otherwise punishment would follow, *for the LORD your God is a consuming fire, a jealous God.*

Fire is a strong reminder of God's judgment. For God's people there will be a day of judgment when a person's *work will be shown for what it is . . . It will be revealed with fire, and the fire will test the quality of each man's work* (1 Corinthians 3:13).

Work that is likened to *wood, hay or straw,* will be *burned up* (3:15). For unbelievers, God's judgment will come *in flaming fire, inflicting vengeance on those who do not know God,* (2 Thessalonians 1:7,9).

Reflection: *We displease God by false worship, being ungrateful and worshipping without due regard for who he is. We should "worship God acceptably with reverence and awe for our God is a consuming fire".*

THE LORD IS MY HELPER
(Hebrews 13:5, 6, quoted from Psalm 118:6, 7)

WHEN THE EARLY CHURCH became distinct from Judaism it lost its legal protection in the Roman Empire and Christians were sometimes subject to persecution. These Jewish Christians therefore needed to support each other so their attitudes, the problem of greed, and a love of money were issues affecting relationships with others.

They were to be content with what they had (Hebrews 13:5), because the Lord had promised, *Never will I leave you . . . Therefore, the Lord is my helper; I will not be afraid.*

It is not easy for anyone to be without fear in time of difficulty, but about sixty-five times in the Bible people are told by God, *Do not be afraid*. Therefore, with the Lord as *my Helper* we can face the difficulties of life and not be terrorized by the events that occur around us.

Reflection: *Knowing the "Lord is my Helper" gives me confidence to get on with my life without fear, while enjoying the contentment of his provision.*

THE FATHER OF THE HEAVENLY LIGHTS
(James 1:17)

JAMES IN REFERRING TO God as the *Father of Heavenly Lights* contrasts the variation that occurs in nature with the consistency in the way God acts.

The earth as part of God's creation rotates and there is a change from night to day. The shadows change according to the position of the sun. The length of the day varies according to the seasons, the moon waxes and wanes throughout the month and the stars vary in their positions and brightness.

But, the *Father of heavenly lights* himself *does not change like shifting shadows,* and as the prophet recorded, *I the Lord do not change* (Malachi 3:6). The actions of God are therefore entirely consistent with his unchanging character and James wanted these scattered Christians to be assured of this.

Reflection: *The "Father of heavenly lights" created and sustains a universe with all its in-built variation. God is not capricious in his actions, so we should be encouraged to trust him as we pray.*

THE ONE LAWGIVER AND JUDGE

(James 4:12)

As THE *LAWGIVER*, GOD gave the law to Moses in order to reveal the holiness of his character to his people. The law set the standard for their behavior and if Israel obeyed the law this would mean a holy lifestyle, fellowship with God and the enjoyment of his blessings.

But the law had to be upheld if it was to have meaning, and so God was both *Lawgiver and Judge*. To break the law meant sin and the need for people to be restored in their relationship with God through sacrifice. Obeying the law was in Israel's best interests, distinguishing them from the nations as God's holy people.

James wanted to remind these Jewish Christians of this understanding of God as a *Lawgiver and Judge*, and taught them (chapter 4) to be careful how they talked and behaved.

Reflection: *We have "one Lawgiver and Judge" who has now entrusted all judgment to the Son (John 5:22). Be careful how you speak and act towards others.*

THE ONE WHO IS ABLE TO SAVE AND DESTROY

(James 4:12)

As *LAWGIVER AND JUDGE*, God gave his law to Israel and governed them through Moses.

The One who is able to save and destroy, is an expansion of this title as it outlines the extended powers of the *Lawgiver and Judge*.

As the *One who is able to save*, God rescues and restores his people to himself. He did this for the world when he sent his Son as Savior (John 3:16). There are people who are *condemned already* (John 3:18), because they do not recognize God's provision for them in Christ.

God acts in accordance with his character of love and holiness. As a God of love he provided salvation consistent with his holiness. But as a holy God he has to take action against those who do not respond to his love.

Reflection: *Knowing the future of your friends who do not love God is a strong incentive for you to share the gospel with them.*

A FAITHFUL CREATOR
(1 Peter 4:19)

IN THE YEARS THAT followed the crucifixion of the Lord Jesus, the Christians in Jerusalem were persecuted. Peter explained to these Christians who had been scattered throughout Asia Minor that suffering was to be expected. Jesus had earlier told his disciples that they would be persecuted (John 15:20), so to *suffer according to God's will* was part of his design for them as their *faithful Creator*.

In responding to their suffering, Peter told them to *commit themselves to their faithful Creator*. The word *commit* has the idea of a person entrusting something of value to a close friend for safe keeping. In Jewish society a breach of such a trust was unthinkable.

With the assurance from a *faithful Creator* who was guarding the "deposit" of their lives, they could be confident and *continue to do good* and avoid the danger of pulling back through fear.

Reflection: *A blessing that comes from difficult circumstances is to know that our "faithful Creator" can be trusted.*

THE GOD OF ALL GRACE
(1 Peter 5:10)

PETER WROTE TO JEWISH Christians who had left Jerusalem to escape persecution and were now living in Asia Minor. In contrast to the gods of this region that were thought to act spitefully, Peter contrasted the generosity of our God by using the title, *the God of all grace*.

God's grace had come to his people as a free and undeserved gift in Christ, through whom they received forgiveness of sin and salvation. Peter explained that in the midst of hardships it is the *God of all grace* who strengthened them.

Further, it is the *God of all grace* who will *restore you and make you strong, firm and steadfast*, (5:10). The word *restore* has the idea of getting a person through difficulties and of repairing the damage caused by suffering. He is a God who can establish, strengthen, and empower our lives too.

Reflection: *"Restore us again, O God of our salvation, and put away your indignation toward us" (Psalm 85:4).*

THE MAJESTIC GLORY
(2 Peter 1:17)

THE LORD HAD TAKEN Peter, James and John on a mountain climb with a difference, for that day their Lord was transfigured before them (Matthew 17:2). The disciples were terrified by what they heard and saw and fell face down to the ground (17:6).

Some years later, the events of that day were still vivid in Peter's mind. He wrote that the voice of God had conveyed *honor and glory* to his Son. This confirmed that the Son was within the love and pleasure of the Father's will (2 Peter 1:17).

By now the terrifying nature of the experience had faded, but the event had made its impact. What the three disciples had once thought was a voice from heaven was none other than the voice of the *Majestic Glory*. God had spoken and Peter knew that his Lord had been honored by his heavenly Father.

Reflection: *The "Majestic Glory" still speaks through his Word and by his Holy Spirit to bring honor to his Son. Are you listening?*

THE ONLY GOD OUR SAVIOR
(Jude 24)

JUDE CLOSES HIS LETTER with a song of praise to *the only God our Savior*. This phrase indicates that God planned our salvation. It was God who *so loved the world that he gave his Son* (John 3:16). The use of the word *only* emphasizes that of the many gods and deities that attract the worship of men and women, there is only one God who is the Savior of the world.

While there are many religions each claiming to have knowledge of the truth, Jude made it clear *that all glory, honor, dominion and majesty* is due to *the only God our Savior*.

Truth by its very nature is exclusive. Therefore, the knowledge that salvation is only found in *God our Savior* through *Jesus Christ our Lord* (v.25) means that other religions give only a false hope.

Reflection: *"To him belongs eternal praise" (Psalm 111:10). Make it your aim to live each day to the glory and praise of God our Savior.*

HE WHO IS AND WHO WAS AND WHO IS TO COME
(Revelation 1:4)

JOHN'S OPENING GREETING TO the seven churches in Asia in the book of Revelation is from the triune God. God the Father is named as *he who is, and who was, and who is to come*. The Holy Spirit is referred to as the *seven spirits before his throne*, and there is *Jesus Christ* God's Son. John referred to God in his eternity in the present, the past and the future.

As to the present, God loves us in Christ (Revelation 1:5).
As to the past he raised Christ as *the first born from the dead* (1:5).
As to the future he is deserving of all *glory and power for ever and ever* (1:6, 7).

Reflection: *What a future we have to know that one day "the dwelling of God will be with men, and he will live with them. They will be his people, and God himself will be with them and be their God" (Revelation 21:3).*

THE KING OF THE AGES/NATIONS
(Revelation 15:3)

SOMETIMES THE "AGES OF Man" are known by the materials used at that period of time. For instance, there was the Stone Age and the Iron Age and there is our present Information Age.

Other periods of history are known by the name of the dominant nation that ruled, such as the Roman Empire. But the *Lord God Almighty* is the *King of the Ages and Nations* that dominate each period of history.

For God to have this title means that he has all authority and power over events both in the past, the present and the future. The title forms part of a song of praise recognizing God because of his *great and marvelous works* and his *ways* which are *righteous and true*.

Reflection: *In spite of man's sinfulness, God has had his plan throughout the ages to draw people to himself. We can be certain that our lives and the future of the world are safe in the care of the "King of the Ages".*

Names for, and References to, God the Father

I AM THE ALPHA AND THE OMEGA—THE ALMIGHTY
(Revelation 1:8)

ALPHA AND OMEGA ARE the first and last letters of the Greek alphabet and refer to God as the Lord of history. The title is a metaphor for the Lord Jesus (Revelation 22:13), but in the above verse it is used for God the Father.

The description of *the Almighty* as the *Alpha and the Omega, who is, and who was, and who is to come,* identifies something of the eternal existence and greatness of God.

As these titles embrace the "I AM" name that the Lord first revealed to Moses (Exodus 3:14), we see that he is still the same eternally existing and unchanging Lord, the *Alpha and the Omega, the Almighty.*

Reflection: *Knowing that the "I AM" is "the Alpha and the Omega– the Almighty" should give us confidence to believe that God has the future in his control. We too should worship with John, "To him be glory and power for ever and ever, Amen".*

THE MIGHTY ONE
(Luke 1:49)

THIS NAME OCCURS IN the song of Mary on the occasion of her visit to her cousin Elizabeth.

The angel Gabriel had previously told Mary that she was to give birth to the *Son of the Most High* (1:32). She was also told that her cousin Elizabeth was to have a child within three months, (1:36–38).

Mary had accepted this word from the angel, but you can imagine the excitement and the turmoil in her mind as she hurried to be with her cousin and confide in her the detail of this angelic revelation.

So Mary in her song of praise was using a name for God which emphasized the demonstration of his power in giving her a child in what seemed impossible circumstances. But as the angel had already reminded her, *nothing is impossible with God* (Luke 1:37).

Reflection: *The "Mighty One" had chosen Mary to be the mother of Jesus and so Christmas is a celebration of the work of the "Mighty One".*

THE LORD GOD ALMIGHTY
(Revelation 19:6, 7)

EACH OF THE SIX mentions of the name, *the Lord God Almighty* in the book of Revelation has a focus on worship.

- First, the four living creatures are day and night saying *"Holy, holy, holy is the Lord God Almighty,* (4:8).
- There are also the twenty-four elders who fall on their faces saying, *"We give thanks to you, Lord God Almighty* (11:17).
- Then there were those who were victorious over *the beast and his image,* who worship as they sing the song of Moses and the song of the Lamb. *Great and marvelous are your deeds, Lord God Almighty.* (15:3).
- Similar words are also repeated from the altar in response to the angel, *Yes, Lord God Almighty, true and just are your judgments* (16:7).
- Finally, John noted that the new Jerusalem has no temple, for *the Lord God Almighty and the Lamb are its temple* (21:22).

Reflection: *In the New Jerusalem we will enter the presence of "the Lord God Almighty", gaze upon his glory, and worship him for all eternity.*

THE LORD, THE GOD OF THE HEBREWS
(Exodus 7:16)

THE EGYPTIANS FIRST USED the term "Hebrews" for migrant workers in their country but later the word became the ethnic name of the Jewish people. The title *The Lord, the God of the Hebrews* only occurs in the book of Exodus and provides the authority for approaching Pharaoh to release God's people from slavery.

"Israel" was the name given by God to Jacob (Genesis 32:28) and Jacob's descendants referred to God as *the Lord, the God of Israel* (e.g. Joshua 8:30).

What a difference a name can make. To the Egyptians they were Hebrews, a downtrodden people working as slaves. But all the time they were Israel, God's chosen people whom he wanted to bless. As the Children of Israel, they needed to change their image of themselves.

Reflection: *Remember we too are "a chosen people, a royal priesthood, a holy nation, a people belonging to God" (1 Peter 2:9). What a difference this should make to the image we have of ourselves.*

THE LORD OF HOSTS
(Malachi 3:1, 17)

IN MALACHI 3 IT is the Lord of Hosts (Armies or Lord Almighty-NIV) who announces the coming of his *messenger*, (John the Baptist), who will prepare the way for the Messiah. The title emphasizes the Lord's absolute power, and in this instance, his control over events associated with Messiah's coming.

Chapter 2:17 asks the question, *Where is the God of Justice?"* Now in chapter 3 we have the answer. Messiah is spoken of as the *messenger of the covenant, . . . coming to his temple* (verse 1) as a *delight* to some, but to others as a day of judgement . . . *who can endure the day of his coming?*

His judgement is spoken of as a *refiner's fire, a fuller's soap, and a smelter and purifier of sliver,* (v.2-3). This judgement views the restoration of his people, who will present *offerings of righteousness,* (v 3).

Reflection: *His invitation is still the same today*: "Return to me and I will return to you, says the Lord of Hosts" (3:7).

THE BLESSED AND ONLY RULER
(1 Timothy 6:15)

A RULER IS SOMEONE who governs or judges and in the Bible both God the Father and the Lord Jesus are given the title of "Ruler". The word has the idea of being first in order by rank and so God has this position and authority for as *the blessed and only Ruler*, he is *King of kings and Lord of lords,* (1 Timothy 6:15).

Throughout history rulers have often been tyrants but Paul recognizes God as deserving of recognition as the *Blessed and Only Ruler* with authority over all other kings and rulers.

His leadership of Israel through Moses and others and his sending of Jesus Christ as a Sacrifice for the sin of the world makes him deserving of *"all honor and eternal dominion"* (v16).

Reflection: *But God has made us rulers over the works of his hands (Psalm 8:4–9). What a responsibility is assigned to us in being stewards over his creation and what a responsibility it is not to spoil his handiwork.*

THE DEW OF ISRAEL

I will heal their waywardness and love them freely . . . I will be like the dew to Israel, (Hosea 14:4, 5).

IN A DRY HOT land the morning dew sometimes provides the much-needed moisture that keeps the vegetation alive. It is this picture of refreshment and blessing that the prophet has in mind when he used this unusual simile for God as being like the *dew to Israel.*

In contrast the love of Israel for God is likened to *the morning mist, like the early dew that disappears* (13:3). This picture indicated a love for God that had evaporated through their disobedience (9:17).

Now in the final chapter of the book there is the assurance, that if they would return to him, the Lord would be *like the dew to Israel,* refreshing a spiritually dry nation.

Reflection: *We all need the "refreshing dew" of the Lord's presence in our lives, so "let us press on to acknowledge him", (Hosea 6:3).*

Names for, and References to, God the Son, our Lord Jesus Christ

A SHOOT
(Isaiah 11:1)

THE MESSIAH IS REFERRED to as *a Shoot*, which *will come up from the stump of Jesse* (Isaiah 11:1). The mention of a *"stump"* indicates that only a remnant of the family tree remained. Israel and Judah faced a coming exile (Isaiah 8:7, 8; 13:4, 5), so against this picture of despair the image of a *shoot* gave hope that new life would again sprout from the old *stump*.

But Isaiah also saw the humble circumstances of Jesus' childhood for he said, *He grew up before him like a tender shoot, and like a root out of dry ground . . .* (Isaiah 53:2). From this unlikely *dry ground* of a downtrodden Jewish society under the rule of the Romans the *tender shoot, the Root of Jesse* would draw all men to himself, (John 12:32).

Reflection: *"A root out of dry ground"—do these words describe you and your prospects in life? God continues to take unlikely people and raise them to effectively serve him.*

MY SERVANT
(Isaiah 42:1)

THE TERM "SERVANT" IN the book of Isaiah refers to both the nation of Israel and to the promised Messiah, *my chosen one*. Although God chose Israel as a servant, the people failed to fulfill his purposes so *my servant* the Messiah was sent to redeem Israel (Luke 1:68).

In Isaiah 42:1–9, *my Servant* is described in his humility and concern for the poor (42:2), and the hurting or broken person, (42:3). The prophet also envisaged the triumph of *my Servant* in his great achievements and widespread influence, (42:4). Further, he would be a *covenant for the people and a light for the Gentiles, to open eyes that are blind, to free captives from prison* (42:6, 7).

Years later the Jewish people had great trouble interpreting these Servant passages for they could not understand that the coming of Messiah was for the benefit of the nations of the whole world.

Reflection: *The Lord Jesus beautifully fulfilled these Servant prophecies and today he continues to set people free from every nation.*

THE SON OF THE MOST HIGH
(Luke 1:32, 33)

FOR MARY TO BE told by the angel that she would give birth to the *Son of the Most High* was for her to know that she would become the earthly mother of God's Son. The name *God Most High* (El Elyon) was an Old Testament name indicating God's preeminence over all. Mary must have felt overwhelmed at what was soon to happen to her.

Mary would have known Joseph's ancestral connection with King David, but for her son to have the *throne of his father David* as a never ending reign over the nation (*the house of Jacob)* would mean nothing less than giving birth to the Messiah.

You can imagine her trembling excitement as she went to visit her cousin Elizabeth (Luke 1:39, 40).

Reflection: *The Son of the Most High still takes up residence in our lives today by his Holy Spirit. Do not take his presence for granted but like Mary glorify the Lord and rejoice in God our Savior, (Luke 1:46-47).*

MY RIGHTEOUS SERVANT
(Isaiah 53:11)

MY RIGHTEOUS SERVANT was none other than the Son of God who humbled himself and was born to this earth in obedience to the will of his Father. Being God in human form, his birth to the virgin Mary ensured that he retained his sinless nature, while in his life the integrity of his righteous character was seen in all that he did.

In referring to the coming Messiah as *My Righteous Servant,* Isaiah anticipated the holiness of his life and his obedience to his Father's will. But obedience to his Heavenly Father meant that he would also become a Suffering Servant and his readiness to suffer was most obvious when he faced his crucifixion.

In the words of his prayer to his Father his righteous obedience was evident when he said, *not my will, but yours be done* (Luke 22:42).

Reflection: *As believers in Jesus as our Lord and Savior we too are declared righteous and are called as servants to obey him.*

THE CONSOLATION OF ISRAEL

(Luke 2:25)

THE OLD TESTAMENT PROPHECIES of a coming Messiah were well known at the time of Jesus' birth but there were very few people who recognized him at his coming.

On the day that Joseph and Mary presented Jesus at the temple, Simeon had been prompted by the Holy Spirit to be there. On seeing the baby he immediately recognized Messiah, *the Consolation of Israel,* had come who would encourage, bring strength and make his appeal to the people.

Taking the child in his arms, Simeon praised God and prophesied salvation for both the Gentile nations and for Israel (Luke 2:29–32).

Reflection: *Simeon's life was characterized by his righteous devotion while he waited, watched and prayed for the coming of Messiah, "the Consolation of Israel". We too await the coming of the Lord Jesus for his Church, so how do you approach that day? "You ought to live holy and godly lives as you look forward to the day of God and speed its coming" (2 Peter 3:11, 12).*

THE CHRIST—MESSIAH

(John 20:31)

THE TERM *THE CHRIST,* or Anointed One, also means Messiah. Some of the writing prophets of the Old Testament had spoken about the coming of someone who would reign on David's throne bringing peace to the nation (Isaiah 9:7). This Anointed One would be born in Bethlehem (Micah 5:2), and as a great national leader he would reign with justice (Isaiah 11:4).

In the New Testament the Apostle John noted that John the Baptist saw himself as a forerunner to *Christ's* coming (John 3:28).

Jesus too claimed the title of *Jesus Christ* (John 17:3) and John declared that his purpose for writing the gospel was *that you may believe that Jesus is the Christ the Son of God and that by believing you may have life in his name* (John 20:31).

Reflection: *As Christians we know him by this name, for we are "believers in our glorious Lord Jesus Christ" (James 2:1), and have "the grace of our Lord Jesus Christ" with us (Galatians 6:18).*

THE CHOSEN ONE

He saved others; let him save himself if he is the Christ of God, the Chosen One, (Luke 23:35).

LUKE RECORDED THAT THE Jewish rulers spoke these words about the Lord Jesus in a sneering manner as he hung on the cross.

Unwittingly they had spoken the truth about Jesus and demonstrated their knowledge of the Old Testament by linking the title *the Christ of God* with the title, the *Chosen One*, for Isaiah recorded, *Here is my servant, whom I uphold, my chosen one in whom I delight* (Isaiah 42:1).

The Jewish rulers understood about the promise of a coming Messiah, but they were entrenched in their positions of national leadership and saw the claims of Christ as a threat to their power. They therefore chose not to accept his claim to deity, but rather have him crucified.

Reflection: *We too have been chosen by God, "Therefore as God's chosen people, holy and dearly loved, clothe yourselves with compassion, kindness, humility, gentleness and patience" (Colossians 3:12).*

THE BRANCH

(Isaiah 4:2)

THERE ARE THREE OLD Testament writers who prophesized concerning the Lord Jesus as *the Branch* from King David's family tree. In Isaiah 4:2, the reference is to the coming Messiah as *the Branch of the Lord, beautiful and glorious*. This *Branch from the root will bear fruit*, as the Spirit of the Lord rests on Him and he enjoys *wisdom and understanding, counsel and power* (Isaiah 11:1, 2).

For Jeremiah the coming King would be a *righteous Branch* who would reign wisely. Without oppression and injustice both Judah and Israel would be saved (Jeremiah 23:5; 33:15).

Zechariah also spoke about the coming of *my servant the Branch* and emphasized the *removal of sin in a single day* (Zechariah 3:8–9), an event that was accomplished through the Lord's crucifixion. The man whose name is *the Branch, will branch out from his place and build the temple of the Lord* (Zechariah 6:12). This *temple* is a symbol of the body of believers.

Reflection: *Consider how "the Branch" continues to branch out and build his Church around the world.*

HE WHO HAD NO SIN

(2 Corinthians 5:21)

ALL OF US HAVE inherited sin from our parents and so we all have a sinful nature. However, the virgin birth of Christ was God's way of by-passing the sin of the world and sending his Son to earth as a fully human person untouched by sin.

His sinless nature meant that he retained his divinity as a man and was qualified to be the perfect sacrifice for the sins of the world.

The Old Testament law required that an animal for the atonement sacrifice had to be free of any blemishes. Therefore, as God's provision for the atonement of our sin, Peter was able to say, *you were redeemed . . . with the precious blood of Christ, a lamb without blemish or defect,* (1 Peter 1:18, 19).

Reflection: *The virgin birth of Jesus ensured his sinless nature as a man, which in turn qualified him to be the atoning sacrifice for our sin. Because of his death Paul could say, "in him we might become the righteousness of God"—Hallelujah! (2 Corinthians 5:21).*

JESUS CHRIST THE SON OF GOD

(Mark 1:1)

IN REFERRING TO JESUS as the *Christ,* Mark affirmed that Jesus was God's Anointed One, the promised Messiah. But the *Son of God* title in this opening verse also affirmed the deity of Jesus. As God's Son he shared the divine nature of God but was born to earth within the limitations of a man.

Mark's opening words in verse 1, *the beginning of the gospel,* are an echo of the first words from Genesis, *In the beginning God created the heavens and the earth.*

This first beginning saw the physical creation of the universe and fellowship between God and man in the Garden of Eden. This next beginning recorded by Mark was also a new beginning, for it again saw God establishing fellowship with men and women but this time through his Son.

Reflection: *"The Son of God has come and has given us understanding so that we may know him who is true" (1 John 5:20). Make it your aim to know him.*

THE SON OF DAVID
(Matthew 15:22)

IN THE BIBLE THE word "son" can mean a descendant from an earlier generation. Jesus was therefore the *Son of David* because he was David's descendant. But the title indicates more.

Old Testament prophecy foretold that a great leader from David's line would be born, (Jeremiah 23:5). The title *Son of David* therefore conveys the idea that this descendant would rule with power and authority. Knowledge that Jesus was the *Son of David* must have been widely understood, for even a Canaanite woman and two blind beggars recognized Jesus as the *Son of David* (Matthew 15:22; 20:30, 31).

Jesus today is building a spiritual kingdom in the hearts of his followers, but as *the Root and the Offspring of David*, (Revelation 22:16), he will one day return and establish his earthly Kingdom (Revelation 21).

Reflection: *Knowing Jesus as "the Son of David" means appreciating his Kingly authority and power over his spiritual kingdom now, and his earthly kingdom in the future. "Hosanna to the Son of David".*

THE SON
Whoever believes in the Son has eternal life, (John 3:36).

WHILE THERE IS ONE true God (Romans 3:30), God has also revealed himself in three distinct persons: God the Father, God the Son and God the Holy Spirit (Matthew 28:19). *The Son* is the title of the God/Man who came to earth *from the Father* (John 1:14).

There is a oneness in the relationship of the Father and the Son (John 10:30). But there is also a dependence of the Son on the Father. *The Son can do nothing by himself; he can do only what he sees his Father doing,* (John 5:19).

The Father loves the Son (John 5:20), and the honor we give to the Father is dependent on knowing and honoring *the Son,* (John 5:23). It is from *God the Son* that we receive salvation, (John 3:36), and it is to the Son that the Father has trusted all judgement, (John 5:22).

Reflection: *Eternal life and freedom, or condemnation and exclusion from God's presence. These are the alternatives we face in accepting or rejecting "the Son".*

THE SON OF GOD

(1 John 5:20)

THE SON OF GOD is a name that expresses the unique relationship of the Lord Jesus to his heavenly Father. John the Baptist learned of this relationship at the baptism of Jesus when the voice from heaven said, *this is my Son, whom I love, with him I am well pleased* (Matthew 3:17).

When the terrified disciples rowed across the lake they too became convinced of his deity, for they worshipped Jesus, saying, *"Truly you are the Son of God"* (Matthew 14:33). For Paul the proof of Jesus' deity was his resurrection, for he records, Jesus *was declared with power to be the Son of God by his resurrection from the dead* (Romans 1:4).

To believe in Jesus is to believe that he is *the Son of God*.

Reflection: *Knowing that it was Jesus, the "Son of God", who died on the cross, assures us of the nature of his perfect sacrifice for the sin of the world, and of his love for us.*

THE SON OF MAN

(John 3:14)

WHEN JESUS USED THIS title *Son of Man*, it was often associated with his suffering.

Jesus reminded people that at his birth it was the *Son of Man* who had *no place to lay his head* (Matthew 8:20). It was the *Son of Man* who was *going to be betrayed* (Matthew 17:22) and it was the *Son of Man* who was to die on the Cross (John 3:14).

But it was Stephen who saw the heavens open and the *Son of Man standing at the right hand of God* (Acts 7:56). The verse indicates that the Lord Jesus has retained his humanity in the glory as *Son of Man*.

So the Church today looks forward to the coming of the *Son of Man. Therefore you also must be ready, for the Son of Man is coming at an hour you do not expect* (Matthew 24:44).

Reflection: *Consider the "Son of Man" from his humble birth, the suffering of the cross, the glory and exultation of heaven, and the promise of his return.*

THE SON OF THE BLESSED ONE
(Mark 14:61)

AT THE TRIAL OF Jesus the high priest challenged Jesus as to whether he was *the Christ, the Son of the Blessed One*. The name, *the Blessed One,* was a way of referring to God without saying his actual name. This Jewish custom of not speaking the Lord's name was due to their fear of breaking the third commandment by misusing his name (Exodus 20:7).

Jesus replied to the question about being *the Son of the Blessed One,* by saying, "I, I am" (ego eimi). This reply was much more than an affirmative "yes", for Jesus had spoken the Greek equivalent of the "I Am" name (YHWH, Exodus 3:14, 15), thus claiming deity for himself. The high priest was deeply shocked and in a rage tore his clothes and charged Jesus with blasphemy (Mark 14:64).

Reflection: *It is only as we believe that Jesus Christ is the Son of God, "the Son of the Blessed One", that we have life in his name (John 20:31).*

THE MIGHTY GOD
(Isaiah 9:6)

THE NAME THE MIGHTY God is usually a reference to God the Father, (Isaiah 10:21), but in the verse above the prophet gave this name to the coming Messiah.

The people thought of Messiah as God's chosen and anointed Leader who would be a King, for *the government will be on his shoulders* (Isaiah 9:6). It was beyond the people's comprehension to think of the Son of God coming to earth and living a servant lifestyle and dying on behalf of his people.

Other passages in Isaiah also present Messiah as a servant, e.g. (52:13, 14), and must have seemed out of character to the people of Isaiah's day. But the weakness and vulnerability of the promised new-born child (verse 6) is presented in contrast to Messiah as the *Mighty God.*

Reflection: *One day his great power will be seen by all. Then "every knee" will bow before him and "every tongue confess that Jesus Christ is Lord to the glory of God the Father" (Philippians 2:10–11).*

WONDERFUL COUNSELOR
(Isaiah 9:6)

ISAIAH REFERRED TO THE coming Messiah as the *Wonderful Counselor, Mighty God, Everlasting Father, Prince of Peace*. These four names indicate that the coming Messiah was to be a King who would reign on David's throne with justice and righteousness (9:7).

The name *Wonderful Counselor* emphasizes the astonishing wisdom of the advice and direction that the Messiah would bring. His counsel is referred to as being a *great light* to people walking in darkness and his coming is likened to the dawning of a light (9:2).

As the *Wonderful Counselor*, Jesus is recognized for the superior wisdom of his teaching. For instance, Matthew recorded that when Jesus came *to his hometown, he began teaching and the people were amazed. Where did this man get this wisdom and these miraculous powers?* (Matthew 13:54).

Reflection: *The "Wonderful Counselor" continues to speak today through his Word, by his Holy Spirit and through the circumstances of our lives. Are we listening and ready to accept his word to us?*

THE EVERLASTING FATHER
(Isaiah 9:6)

ISAIAH'S USE OF THE name *Everlasting Father* for the coming Messiah literally means *Father of Eternity* for he is the Lord and the author of life. In the same way as Abraham became the father of the nation of Israel, so the Messiah was seen as a leader or father of a revitalized Jewish nation.

In the New Testament Jesus fulfilled his role as *Everlasting Father* through his work on the cross, for he became the *author of life* (Acts 3:15). It is through receiving his eternal salvation that we become *children of God* (1 John 3:1) and members of his family (1 Peter 4:17).

God's family in the Old Testament was Israel the nation, but now Gentile believers have been grafted in to form the Church (Romans 11:17), *making both groups one* (Ephesians 2:14).

Reflection: *As the Everlasting Father, Jesus was God and was with God in eternity (John 1:1). What fatherly care he now offers to those who are members of his family.*

THE PRINCE OF PEACE
(Isaiah 9:6–7)

THE FOUR NAMES COUNSELLOR, Mighty God, Everlasting Father and Prince of Peace all describe the coming Messiah in terms of his character and the blessing he would bring. Each of the names are also descriptive of the character of God himself.

The name *Prince of Peace* speaks of his authority to rule wisely and establish peace. The meaning of the name was also clarified by the words that follow, *Of the increase of his government and peace there will be no end.* Thus his endless rule and his expanding kingdom are envisaged. The name also brings together the ideas associated with the other names.

As the *Prince of Peace,* and in order to establish peace, he would give sound advice, exercise his powerful rule with justice, and maintain a fatherly relationship with his people.

Reflection: *To be at peace with God means that we have a relationship with the "Prince of Peace" and can enjoy his advice, his power and his fatherly comfort and care.*

THE AUTHOR OF THEIR SALVATION
God . . . should make the author of their salvation perfect through suffering, (Hebrews 2:10).

IT IS STRANGE FOR us to think of the Lord Jesus as being made *perfect through suffering,* but as long as the Lord Jesus remained in heaven he had no experience of life as man. In becoming man and facing the humiliation and rejection of men, and the suffering and death on the cross, his experience of life on earth was complete.

It was a perfect experience of manhood by the sinless Son of God who was made *sin for us* (2 Corinthians 5:21). He has therefore earned the title, *author of their salvation.*

Hebrews 5:8, 9, notes that the Lord Jesus, *once made perfect, became the source of eternal salvation for all who obey him.*

Reflection: *Both suffering and obedience completed the experience of the Lord Jesus as a man on earth. This experience perfectly fitted him to be the author and source of eternal salvation. Notice that this salvation is "for all who obey him".*

THE MESSENGER OF THE COVENANT
(Malachi 3:1)

THE NATION OF ISRAEL had failed to keep the covenant of law, and Jeremiah had recorded the promise of a new covenant, (Jeremiah 31:31). Much later it was Malachi who provided clues to the fulfillment of this covenant promise.

Two "messengers" are mentioned. There was the promise of *my messenger*, (John the Baptist) *who will prepare the way before me*, (Malachi 4:6). Then there was the *messenger of the covenant*, (the Messiah), referred to as the *Lord* (Adon), meaning a master with authority.

This word "messenger" refers to a supernatural representative of God. The words in Malachi 3:1, *the Lord you are seeking will come to his temple*, express beautifully the expectation of the people as they waited for their Messiah.

Reflection: *Jesus did come to his temple, but at his trial before the High Priest he was accused of blasphemy which led to his crucifixion. Today Jesus still comes to his temple, for our bodies are the temple of the Holy Spirit (1 Corinthians 6:19).*

GOD, THE ONE AND ONLY
(John 1:18)

THE APOSTLE JOHN USED the title *One and Only* five times as a reference to the Lord Jesus, indicating the unique relationship of Jesus to his heavenly Father as he represented him to the world.

The deity of the Lord Jesus is explicitly stated when he is referred to as *God the One and Only who is at the Father's side* (John 1:18). Here the oneness of the Father and the Son and their intimacy and love are expressed within the context of his position in the glory at the Father's side.

John indicated that as recipients of God's love, we must learn to love others for God's nature is love. We read that this is why . . . *he sent his one and only Son into the world that we might live through him* (1 John 4:9).

Reflection: *"That we might live through him". Make that your prayer today for yourself, your family and your Church.*

THE WORD
(John 1:1)

THE TERM "WORD" WAS familiar to both the Jews and the Greeks and meant more than a spoken or written word. For the Jews, God was "the Word" acting in wisdom, e.g. *by wisdom the earth was made* (Proverbs 3:19). For the Greeks *the Word* indicated the reason or mind needed to create an orderly world.

John therefore starts his gospel addressing both Jews and Greeks using the expression *the Word*, to refer to the Lord Jesus:

- *In the beginning was the Word*—speaking of the eternity of the Lord Jesus prior to creation.
- *the Word was with God*—speaking of his presence in the Godhead;
- *the Word was God*—speaking of his essential Deity as God. Then in verse 14 . . .
- *The Word became flesh and made his dwelling among us*—speaking of his humanity.

Reflection: *By using this term "the Word", John had represented Jesus in a culturally relevant way to both Jews and Greeks. We need to do this today.*

THE WORD OF LIFE
(1 John 1:1)

IN JOHN 1:1–14, THE Apostle John used the expression *The Word* to emphasize the deity and humanity of the Lord Jesus.

Now in 1 John 1:1–3, he speaks about *the Word of Life,* to emphasize that the *Word* is a message that can only be understood in terms of the person of the Lord Jesus in his life, death, resurrection and ascension to heaven. The Lord Jesus as the *Word of Life* is therefore the source and giver of life (John 1:12).

The wonderful outcome of receiving this life is that he brings us into fellowship with other believers because we now have a relationship with God himself (1 John 1:3).

Reflection: *The knowledge of this relationship through God's Son—the Word of Life, was a source of great joy to John, and he wanted it to be a source of great confidence to the believers to whom he wrote. These blessings come from the one who is "the Word of Life".*

THE BREAD OF GOD
(John 6:33)

IN THE OLD TESTAMENT the *bread of God* was associated with the "manna" that God provided for the Israelites during the forty years they traveled in the Sinai Peninsula on their way to the Promised Land of Canaan. The manna was the daily evidence of God's provision to feed his people, (Exodus 16:4–7).

By the time of Jesus, there had arisen a belief that when the Messiah arrived he would provide manna for the people. John recorded the miracle of the feeding of the five thousand, (John 6:11–13), but the next day the crowd wanted more.

Jesus was not about to repeat yesterday's miracle, but explained. *It is my Father who gives you the true bread from heaven. For the bread of God is he who comes down from heaven and gives life to the world*, (John 6:32, 33).

Reflection: *The present tense of the word "gives" in John 6:32, indicates that Jesus as the "bread of God" continues to give spiritual life to all who believe.*

SHILOH

The scepter will not depart from Judah, nor the ruler's staff from between his feet, until he (Shiloh) comes to whom it (tribute) belongs and the obedience of the nations is his, (Genesis 49:10).

JACOB SPOKE THESE WORDS prior to his death as a blessing to his son Judah who was given the leadership of the family. The scepter was the symbol of Judah's authority, and *Shiloh* is the future man of peace.

The initial fulfillment of the prophecy came with King David, but it was not until Christ came that the prophecy was finally fulfilled.

Like David, Jesus was from the tribe of Judah and this prophecy is the first in the Bible to indicate the kingly authority of the Messiah and the eternal nature of his kingdom, for *the scepter will not depart from Judah*.

Reflection: *In a future day our Lord Jesus will receive the obedience of the nations, (Revelation 17:14). What a future victory awaits the coming of "Shiloh", the man of peace whose right it is to reign.*

A WITNESS TO THE PEOPLES, A LEADER AND COMMANDER

See, I have made him (David) a witness to the peoples, a leader and commander of the peoples. Surely you will summon nations you know not, (Isaiah 55:4, 5a).

GOD HAD MADE AN *everlasting covenant* with King David that his descendants and his throne would continue as an everlasting kingdom, (2 Samuel 7:16). Isaiah reflects on what God had done for David, and writes about the future fulfillment of the covenant promise through the Messiah.

When Jesus came, he too was a *witness to the peoples* by revealing his heavenly Father to them, (Revelation 3:14). Further, as the *leader and commander of the peoples* Jesus established his authority and his spiritual kingdom in the lives of his followers, (Revelation 5:9).

Reflection: *We have yet to see all nations acknowledge the authority of the Lord Jesus but the day is coming when they will. "At the name of Jesus every knee should bow . . . and every tongue confess that Jesus Christ is Lord" (Philippians 2:10-11).*

A COVENANT FOR THE PEOPLE
(Isaiah 42:6)

ISAIAH SPOKE ABOUT THE coming Messiah as a servant (42:1) who would be a *covenant for the people*. A *covenant* was a form of agreement in which God expressed his purposes for his people, binding himself to bless them. In response, the covenant people were to forsake other gods and worship and obey him.

Old Testament covenant practices prefigured God's new covenant agreement through sending his Son as *a covenant for the people*. With previous covenants, God's people had failed to keep the terms of the covenant agreement by worshiping other gods.

Now in Christ, God renewed his covenant and this time it would not be limited to the Jewish people, but would be with all who would repent and believe (Mark 1:15). The shedding of Christ's blood on the cross sealed the new covenant.

Reflection: *Next time you celebrate Communion think of it as a covenant meal as you remember the Lord in his death for us. Then renew your allegiance to him.*

A LIGHT FOR THE GENTILES

(Isaiah 42:6, 7)

THE JEWISH PEOPLE FROM the days of Isaiah had difficulty reconciling ideas of the Messiah being a *covenant for the people* while also being a *light for the Gentiles.*

The covenants with Abraham and his descendants indicated that God's blessings were exclusive to Israel. *I will be your God and you will be my people,* was the summary statement of these covenants (Jeremiah 7:23). Therefore many people did not understand how the coming Messiah could be *a light for the Gentiles* when the covenants appeared to exclude this possibility.

But God had a plan to extend his light through a new covenant to the Gentiles. At Messiah's birth it was Simeon who recognized the baby Jesus as *a light for revelation to the Gentiles* (Luke 2:32) and Jesus himself was later to declare *I am the light of the world* (John 8:12).

Reflection: *"You are light in the Lord. Live as children of light" (Ephesians 5:8). What a privilege and responsibility it is to reflect his light.*

THE RISING SUN

The rising sun will come to us from heaven, (Luke 1:78).

AT THE BIRTH OF John the Baptist it was his father Zachariah who prophesied about the future ministry of his son as well as the coming of Messiah (Luke 1:67–79).

Of the Messiah he prophesied, he will *give his people the knowledge of salvation through the forgiveness of their sins* (Luke 1:77). Zachariah then described so beautifully Messiah's coming in this metaphor of the *rising sun from heaven.*

Because of the tender mercy of our God, by which the rising sun will come to us from heaven to shine on those living in darkness and in the shadow of death, to guide our feet into the path of peace (1:78).

Reflection: *In the same way that light and darkness cannot coexist, so the Rising Sun, the Light of the World, dispels that spiritual darkness. In reflecting this light, "let your light shine before men, that they may see your good deeds and praise your Father in heaven" (Matthew 5:16).*

THE TRUE LIGHT
(John 1:9)

JOHN'S STATEMENT ABOUT JESUS as the *true light that gives light to every man* (1:9) is based on an Old Testament prophetic Servant passage. There it says, *I will also make you a light for the Gentiles that you may bring my salvation to the ends of the earth* (Isaiah 49:6b).

The coming of Jesus as *the true light* was therefore an open invitation for every person from all nations to come and receive the spiritual *light of life* (John 8:12).

Later, John was to clarify what he meant about the *true light* when he said, *I am writing you a new command . . . its truth is seen in him and you, because the darkness is passing and the true light is already shining. Whoever loves his brother lives in the light* (1 John 2:8, 10).

Reflection: *What confidence John had when he said, "this truth is seen in him and you". Pray that the true light will be seen in you and demonstrated through your love for others today.*

THE LAMB OF GOD
(John 1:29)

ISAIAH WAS THE PROPHET who prefigured the Messiah as the lamb. *He was led as a lamb to the slaughter*, (Isaiah 53:7). As a *guilt-offering* Jesus would be God's provision as a sacrifice for sin, (Isaiah 53:10).

In the New Testament it was John the Baptist who recognized Jesus as *the Lamb of God who takes away the sin of the world*. John here prophesied about the work that Jesus would one day accomplish through his death on the cross. Unlike the daily sacrifice of the lambs at the Temple, Jesus as the perfect *Lamb of God* only had to die once, (Hebrews 7:27).

Peter outlined the effectiveness of this sacrifice when he said, *we were redeemed with the precious blood of Christ, a lamb without blemish or defect* (1 Peter 1:19).

Reflection: *The "Lamb of God" died as a sacrifice to take away the sin of the world. We are now called to live our lives as "living sacrifices" (Romans 12:1).*

A RULER WHO WILL BE THE SHEPHERD
(Matthew 2:6)

THIS TITLE ABOVE IS a quotation from Micah 5:2, and was part of a conversation in which the chief priests and the teachers of the law tell King Herod about the location and significance of Messiah's birth. The conversation was prompted by the arrival in Jerusalem of three wise men who came looking for the newborn king.

It may seem strange to have the words *ruler* and *shepherd* mentioned in the same sentence and referring to the same person, for rulers were often tyrants. But such was the nature of the Messiah, that both his rule and his shepherd-care were complementary behaviors.

So today Jesus continues to demonstrate his love and shepherd-care of his people in the context of his authority as ruler over his Kingdom.

Reflection: *Until the day comes when the Lord will assert his authority as ruler of the kings of the earth, (Revelation 1:5), it is now our responsibility to show his shepherd-care to others who need his love.*

A PROPHET
(Luke 7:16)

FOR A TIME IN Israel's history there were three distinct types of leaders, the prophet, the priest and the king.

The prophet brought the message of God to the people, the priest offered sacrifices and prayers in worship to God, and the King governed the affairs of State as God's representative. This leadership structure foreshadowed the ministry of the Lord Jesus when he came to earth as our Prophet, Priest and King.

The Lord Jesus was a prophet for he spoke the truth about God as well as speaking prophetically about future events, such as his impending death (John 16:16). On most occasions however, the people used the title of prophet because they did not realize who Jesus was, (John 9:17b).

Reflection: *It is significant that in the New Testament epistles Jesus is not spoken about as a prophet because he was more than a prophet. Muslim people today still consider that Jesus was only a prophet. What is your estimate of him?*

A MAN
(John 4:29)

PEOPLE WHO DID NOT know Jesus often referred to him as "*a man*". For instance, the woman from Samaria reported her meeting with him to her fellow townspeople when she said, *Come, see a man who told me everything I ever did. Could this be the Christ?*, (John 4:29).

The words "*man*" emphasizes the humanity of Jesus, for as a man the Son of God had lived among men doing his miracles and teaching the people.

The story of the healing of the blind man illustrates how a person's understanding of Jesus grew from thinking of him as just a man (John 9:11), to referring to him as a prophet (9:17). Later he addressed Jesus respectfully as "Sir" (9:36), and then, when Jesus revealed himself to him, he worshipped him as "Lord" (9:38).

Reflection: *What a difference it makes when we know the divine origin of the man Jesus, but like the blind-man we all need to believe and know him as Lord.*

THE LIVING BREAD
(John 6:51)

THE DAY AFTER JESUS had fed a crowd of more than five thousand with only five barley loaves and two small fish, (6:9), the people remembered what happened in the time of Moses when they had "bread from heaven" or "manna" (Exodus 16:4, 31).

When Jesus said he had come *from heaven* (6:41), the people debated how this could be possible. To clarify the discussion Jesus then said, *I am the bread of life* (6:48). *I am the living bread that came down from heaven. If anyone eats this bread he will live forever* (6:51).

The crowd knew that with some of the temple sacrifices part of the offering was given back to the worshippers to eat with their friends. However, it was beyond their understanding that Jesus could be the *living bread* and give his flesh *for the life of the world*.

Reflection: *Next time you celebrate communion, reflect on the "living bread" that was given for "the life of the world".*

RABBI

(Mark 10:51)

The title "Rabbi" was a form of address that was commonly used for a respected teacher. Each Rabbi had his own students who would live with him and act as his servants in return for their food and teaching. Thus the students would learn the interpretations of the Old Testament Scriptures and the oral and written Jewish traditions.

They would also adopt the attitudes and lifestyle of their teacher. The authority of the Rabbis came from what previous interpreters of the law had said and not from their own opinions.

The teaching of Jesus was unique, for he taught with his own authority and made no attempt to quote other Jewish Rabbis and their interpretations. But when Jesus chose his disciples he did exactly what every Rabbi had done before him. They lived with him and embraced his teaching, his attitudes and his lifestyle.

Reflection: *When Jesus calls us to follow him we too are invited to live in intimate fellowship with him in order to learn from him.*

LORD OF THE SABBATH

(Matthew 12:8)

The Sabbath was a reminder that God was Creator and had redeemed Israel from slavery, (Deuteronomy 5:15). It was also a weekly reminder of their covenant relationship with God. As God's holy people, the Sabbath was a sign between God and his people, *so you may know that I am the Lord who makes you holy* (Exodus 31:13).

By the time of Jesus, Jewish tradition had established an intolerable set of regulations, but Jesus explained that being merciful was more important than making sacrifices. He then proceeded to offend the Pharisees by healing a man with a shriveled hand.

As *Lord of the Sabbath* he demonstrated the principle that it was *lawful to do good on the Sabbath* (Matt.12:9–12); even if this meant breaking their Jewish traditions.

Reflection: *Paul wrote that the "letter (of the law) kills, but the Spirit gives life" (2 Corinthians 3:6). The Lord of the Sabbath brings freedom to do good. Avoid legalism for it is the enemy of our freedom in Christ.*

THE HOLY ONE OF GOD
(John 6:69)

IN JOHN 6, PETER said of Jesus, *you have the words of eternal life and we believe and know that you are the Holy One of God* (6:69).

To "believe" means to trust, but to "know" is to be certain about what you believe and so Peter expressed his absolute confidence in Jesus as the *Holy One of God*. The name *the Holy One* is used forty-four times as a title for God in eight books of the Old Testament. It was therefore a title that was familiar to the disciples.

Peter used this title to refer to Jesus, therefore indicating that he recognized him as having come from God in the fullness of God's character.

Reflection: *Today we can be assured that "we have an anointing from the Holy One and all of you know the truth" (1 John 2:20). Allow the truth of God's word and his anointing to direct and empower you in your service for the "Holy One".*

I, I AM
(John 6:20, 21)

IN EXODUS 3:14, 15, the Lord revealed himself to Moses by the name "I Am Who I AM" (*YHWH*), which is written throughout the Old Testament as "LORD". This was the name by which God wanted to be remembered (Ex.3:15). In the Jewish Septuagint this name was written in Greek as "ego eimi" and later Jesus used this name for himself.

The disciples had seen Jesus turn water into wine and had put their faith in him (John 2:1–11), but as they rowed across a stormy lake at night, they were terrified to see something or someone walking over the water towards them. Then they realized it was Jesus when they heard him speak the name: *"It is I, (I Am) don't be afraid"* (John 6: 20).

Reflection: *On other occasions Jesus also used this name, each time revealing something more about himself. Knowing that the "I Am" is with us and that we don't need to be afraid should be a wonderful source of comfort.*

THE LIGHT OF THE WORLD

(John 8:12)

LIGHT AND DARKNESS ARE associated with day and night, and the saying "to see the light" is a figurative expression referring to understanding something previously unknown.

Jesus said of himself *I Am the light of the world. Whoever follows me will never walk in darkness, but will have the light of life* (John 8:12). The *I Am* name of the Lord in this verse connects the name with *the light,* and highlights the essential purity and holiness of his being. In coming to this world Jesus was the source of light, for he gave understanding of the truth and made holiness a reality for his followers.

To hear and accept the words of Jesus is to receive light, and to follow him is to be delivered from darkness and to have him as *the light of life.*

Reflection: *Living by the truth of God's Word is referred to as "walking in the light" (1 John 1:7-10). Make that your aim today.*

THE BREAD OF LIFE

(John 6:35)

BREAD WAS THE STAPLE food in the time of Jesus and on several occasions he referred to it when talking about what was needed to sustain life.

On the day following the feeding of the five thousand with bread and fish, the crowds were again expecting Jesus to feed them. They wanted a miracle (6:30), so Jesus explained *the bread of God is he who comes down from heaven and gives life to the world* (6:33).

Persisting in their request for bread, Jesus replied *I Am the bread of life.* With these words Jesus laid claim to be God and to be the source of spiritual life, but the people grumbled and disputed his divine origin (6:41, 42). Some followers turned away from following him (6:66), but Peter understood and said, *we believe and know that you are the Holy One of God* (6:69).

Reflection: *Jesus is the "bread of life", the One who gives us life and sustains us as we feed on him.*

THE GATE FOR THE SHEEP
(John 10:7, 8)

ONCE SHEPHERDS IN PALESTINE were either nomadic herdsmen, sleeping out on the hillsides to protect their animals, or village shepherds bringing their sheep each night into a common sheep pen. A stone wall enclosure or a wall of prickly bushes would keep wild animals away from attacking the sheep. Each sheep had a name and each morning the sheep would recognize the call of their shepherd to follow him.

In reminding the Pharisees of this common farming practice, Jesus highlighted the difference between the shepherd who approached the sheep pen via the gate, and the thief who climbed over the wall to steal the sheep.

At this point Jesus declared his divine name, *"I Am" the gate for the sheep* (John 10:9, 10).

Reflection: *Knowing Jesus as "the gate for the sheep" is to know him as the only way to eternal life. Entry through the gate is to experience his care, protection and the freedom to "come in and out and find pasture".*

THE GOOD SHEPHERD
(John 10:11)

IN NEW TESTAMENT TIMES the work of a shepherd required long lonely hours on the hillsides caring for the sheep. It was demeaning work because sheep required attention seven days a week and shepherds could not observe the Jewish Sabbath rest.

However, in a pastoral countryside, sheep were a form of wealth that could be sold for income, provide animals for sacrifice and food for the family.

As the *good shepherd*, Jesus indicated that he valued his followers (sheep) so highly that he would *lay down his life for the sheep*, with the authority (from his Father) to die and rise again (John 10:11, 17, 18). He also foreshadowed the extension of his flock to include *other sheep* (10:16) indicating that non-Jewish people would also become his followers belonging to one flock.

Reflection: *Today there are still those who are hostile to the claims of Jesus, and "wolves" that attack the sheep and shepherds who run away. However, true sheep know the voice of the "good Shepherd" who cares for them.*

Names for, and References to, God the Son, our Lord Jesus Christ

THE LORD
(Luke 24:34)

The name the disciples used most often in speaking of Jesus was the title of *Lord*. This name brought together the meanings of the two Hebrew names of *YHWH* and *Adonai*.

YHWH, or LORD, means the self-existent one who is always present and in covenant relationship with his people, and *Adonai*, or *Lord*, means Sovereign or Master. When the disciples used the name "Lord" they therefore recognized that Jesus was God's Son to whom they had given their allegiance.

People coming to Jesus for help often referred to him as "Lord" as a term of respect, but at his birth he had been given the name "Jesus" or "Joshua", and he was known by this name in his community at Nazareth.

However, to his disciples and followers he was always their *Lord* (John 11:21).

Reflection: *While there are people today who refuse to acknowledge Jesus as their Lord, one day "every knee will bow and confess that Jesus Christ is Lord to the glory of God the Father" (Philippians 2:10, 11).*

THE RESURRECTION AND THE LIFE
(John 11:25)

The evidence that Jesus was *the resurrection and the life,* was his ability to bring the dead back to life. For instance, he sent a message to John the Baptist in prison that he had healed the sick, preached good news to the poor and raised the dead, (Matthew 11:5).

Specifically, Jesus raised the widow of Nain's son to life, (Luke 7:11–15), as well as Lazarus (John 11:38–44). But the ultimate proof that Jesus was Lord of life with power over death was his own resurrection (John 20:1–18).

One day we will all experience a resurrection (Acts 24:15), and for those who love the Lord this will mean our transformation into his likeness, for *we know that when he appears we shall be like him, for we shall see him as he is* (1 John 3:2).

Reflection: *As "children of the resurrection" (Luke 20:36), we have his resurrection power with us today, (Romans 8:11). What a difference this should make to the way we live.*

THE WAY THE TRUTH AND THE LIFE
(John 14:6)

JESUS HAD TOLD HIS disciples that he would only be with them for a little longer, (John 13:31–38), to which Thomas reacted, *Lord we don't know where you are going, so how can we know the way?* (14:5). It was then that Jesus declared his name as *I, I am (ego eimi), the way the truth and the life.* With this metaphor Jesus revealed himself as Lord of the way, the Lord of truth and the Lord of life.

As "the Way", Jesus declared all other gods as false religions for there is no other way to the Father than through him.

As "the Truth", Jesus claimed to be the truth and to reveal the truth about God.

As "the Life", Jesus is the source of life to those who believe in him (John 5:24–26).

Reflection: *As "the way, the truth and the life", Jesus continues to lead us, revealing his truth to us and sustaining us in our spiritual lives.*

YOUR LORD AND TEACHER
(John 13:14)

JESUS WAS OFTEN REFERRED to by the title of *Teacher,* and sometimes by the more prestigious title of Rabbi, but Jesus never referred to himself as a Rabbi. Using the title of "Lord and Teacher" he washed his disciple's feet and demonstrated to them an example of humble service which he expected them to follow.

As a teacher, Jesus sometimes taught in the Synagogues, (Matthew 4:23). Most often however, his classroom was the countryside or village setting where he taught the crowds and performed his miracles. It was there that the disciples witnessed their *Lord and Teacher* in action.

When Jesus taught, he demonstrated a personal authority, (Mark 1:22). In contrast, the teachers of the law had an authority based on the interpretations of past scholars but everything that Jesus said was fresh and original.

Reflection: *Learning from Jesus means becoming a disciple and involves personal discipline, a gentle and humble nature and a daily walk in which we enjoy the refreshment of his presence.*

MY LORD AND MY GOD
(John 20:28)

THOMAS IS OFTEN REMEMBERED as a doubter, but we must also remember him for his courage and devotion. On the occasion when Jesus wanted to return to Bethany in Judea to see the body of Lazarus, the disciples were alarmed, for previously the people had tried to stone him (John 11:8).

Thomas said, *Let us also go, that we may die with him* (11:16). His commitment and courage in a dangerous situation shines through in wanting to go with his Lord. Then, when Jesus appeared to the group of his disciples following his resurrection, Thomas was absent and would not believe when told about what happened, (20:24, 25).

Later when Jesus appeared again, he showed Thomas the nail prints in his hands. The Lord chided him for his doubt, but Thomas responded, *My Lord and my God* thus indicating his devotion to his Lord.

Reflection: *To own Jesus as "my Lord and my God" indicates a personal devotion to Jesus as Lord, accompanied by courage to serve him.*

THE ONE GREATER THAN JONAH, THE ONE GREATER THAN SOLOMON
(Matthew 12:41, 42)

JONAH HAD GONE TO the Assyrian city of Nineveh to bring a message of impending judgment, and there the people had listened and repented (Jonah 3:5–10). But now *one greater than Jonah* was speaking, but his listeners wanted a miracle and not his message.

Jesus then referred to the Queen of Sheba who traveled a great distance to learn from the wisdom of King Solomon (1 Kings 10), but the people again would not accept Jesus as *one greater than Solomon*.

Jesus therefore warned them, that in a future day of judgment, it would be the men of Nineveh and the Queen of Sheba who would speak condemnation against them for not accepting his authority.

Reflection: *The people of Nineveh and the Queen of Sheba were non-Jewish people who had used their limited opportunities to learn about God. It is a sobering thought to realize that their example will be used in judgment against those who refused to accept the testimony of Jesus.*

THE BRIDEGROOM
(Luke 5:34)

A GLIMPSE OF JEWISH wedding customs is seen in the parable of the ten virgins (Matthew 25:1–13). Towards evening of the wedding day the bridegroom with his friends would approach the home of the bride, carrying their lamps while singing and playing their instruments. The bride and her friends would be waiting excitedly and upon arrival, everybody would return to the bridegroom's home singing as they went.

Luke 5:34, presents another wedding scene where Jesus defended his disciples for not fasting because his presence was like being at a wedding celebration and fasting was inappropriate. Jesus then indicated that *the time will come when the Bridegroom will be taken from them* (5:35).

The Church today awaits the return of *the Bridegroom*. His coming will be followed by another grand occasion, *the wedding of the Lamb*, (Revelation 19:7).

Reflection: *The parable of the ten virgins, and the wedding scene from Revelation, highlight the certainty of the Bridegroom's return, our need to be ready and the grandeur of that occasion.*

THE CHRIST OF GOD
(Luke 9:20)

JESUS MODELED HIS TEACHING through his lifestyle and miracles as he preached to the crowds. But when he was alone with his disciples he was able to assess their understanding of him and to explain details about himself and his kingdom.

On one such occasion he asked his disciples who people considered him to be. They replied that they thought of him as either John the Baptist, or Elijah, or an Old Testament prophet risen from the dead. When Peter was asked his opinion his brief reply was *"The Christ of God"*.

Peter had passed the test, so Jesus now explained that an understanding of him meant being a follower who adopted his lifestyle by living unselfishly (9:23). This next lesson was not so easy to learn.

Reflection: *To know the "Christ of God" means knowing that Christ was sent by God to establish his followers in his kingdom and to help them adopt his lifestyle. Being part of his kingdom has lifestyle implications for us today.*

A FRIEND OF TAX COLLECTORS AND SINNERS
(Luke 7:34)

When the Romans governed Palestine they levied taxes on the people's land and their production and sale of goods. The right to raise taxes was auctioned in each district and these tax collectors or "publicans" had to pay a large deposit in advance to the Romans. Frequently the tax collectors employed subcontractors to collect tax in a local area and gained extra income by over-taxing the people.

It is easy to imagine how the community would despise these tax collectors as traitors to Rome. Further, for Jesus to be seen as a *friend of tax collectors and sinners* meant that he too was despised for associating with these people.

Underlying this criticism however, was a deeper problem of their rejection of the message that Jesus taught. Jesus had said, *the Pharisees and experts in the law rejected God's purpose for themselves* (7:30).

Reflection: *If we fail to understand God's purposes we too are likely to become critical of how God is building his Kingdom.*

KING OF THE JEWS
(John 18:33)

Pilate asked Jesus at his trial, *Are you the king of the Jews?* (John 18:33), to which Jesus gave his affirmation, (18:37). Pilate also used this title to bargain about the release of Jesus or Barabbas (18:39, 40), and the soldiers used the title to mock Jesus (19:3). Then for the wording on the cross, Pilate insisted on the title, *Jesus of Nazareth, the King of the Jews.* (19:19).

The title of king had been used by Pilate to taunt the Jews and by the soldiers to show their disdain for Jesus, but little did they realize the nature of his kingship.

The day has yet to come when Jesus will be revealed in his full glory. It is then that his kingly authority will be recognized by all, and not just *as king of the Jews,* but as KING OF KINGS AND LORD OF LORDS (Revelation 19:16).

Reflection: *Today many people seek the meaning of life but reject at their peril "the one who has been born king" (Matthew 2:2).*

THE ONE WHO WAS GOING TO REDEEM ISRAEL
(Luke 24:20b, 21)

THIS REFERENCE TO JESUS forms part of a conversation between two disciples and Jesus as they walked towards a village called Emmaus. They did not realize at the time that it was Jesus who was with them, but felt the blessing of his presence. *"Were not our hearts burning within us while he talked with us on the road?"* (Luke 24:32).

It was Paul however, who saw the significance of Christ's death in terms of our "redemption" for he said, we are *justified freely by his grace through the redemption that came by Christ Jesus* (Romans 3:24).

To the Ephesians, Paul noted that it was *redemption through his blood* (Ephesians 1:7), and to the Colossians he explained the result. *We have redemption, the forgiveness of sins* (Colossians 1:14).

Reflection*: In the Old Testament it is God who is referred to as our Redeemer (Isaiah 47:4) and as our Redeemer he sent his Son to pay the price for our redemption, (1 Corinthians 7:23); Hallelujah.*

A MAN OF SORROWS
(Isaiah 53:3)

"MAN OF SORROWS" is a title that summarizes the physical, mental and emotional sufferings that the Messiah would one day endure, being rejected as Israel's anointed leader. Meditate on the following references:

- *Who, being in very nature God . . . he made himself nothing, taking the very nature of a servant* (Philippians 2:6–7).
- They *drove him out of the town . . . in order to throw him down the cliff* (Luke 4:29).
- The Pharisees . . . *were sneering at Jesus* (Luke 16:14).
- *Even his own brothers did not believe in him* (John 7:5).
- Jesus himself acknowledged *he must suffer many things and be rejected by this generation* (Luke 17:25).
- *Many of them said, "He is demon-possessed and raving mad. Why listen to him?"* (John 10:20).
- Pilate *had Jesus flogged, and handed him over to be crucified* (Matthew 27:26).
- *Jesus cried out, "My God, my God, why have you forsaken me?"* (Mark 15:34).

Reflection: *Contemplating the sufferings of our Lord should make us thankful for what he endured for us.*

Names for, and References to, God the Son, our Lord Jesus Christ

THE CHRIST, THE SON OF THE LIVING GOD
(Matthew 16:15, 16)

THESE VERSES RECORD AN exchange between Jesus and his disciples in the area of Caesarea Philippi. The place had many reminders of early religions.

Nearby were the ancient Syrian temples for the worship of Baal. The River Jordan was a reminder of Jewish history. A cave on the hillside was associated with the Greek god Pan and many Greek myths, and a Roman temple honored Caesar as a god.

Against these reminders of ancient religious faith, Jesus asked the question, *who do people say the Son of Man is* (16:13)? It was as if Jesus was asking his disciples to compare him to these ancient religions.

Several answers were given, but when he asked the question, *but what about you? Who do you say I am?* Peter replied affirmatively. *You are the Christ, the Son of the living God.* Jesus now committed to Peter the task of building his Church (16:18).

Reflection: *Like Peter our understanding of our Lord should lead to active Christian service.*

THE PHYSICIAN
(Luke 4:23)

JESUS HAD TWO HOME towns. There was his boyhood home in Nazareth and the town of Capernaum, where he ministered. When he later returned to these hometowns the reaction of the people was startlingly different.

At Capernaum they gathered to hear him preach and brought their sick for him to heal (Mark 2:1–4). He delivered a man possessed by an evil spirit, healed the Centurion's servant and the paralytic man. Peter's mother-in-law was healed and he restored life to the daughter of Jairus.

In contrast, when Jesus returned to Nazareth the people at the synagogue were surprised at his speaking ability, but they wanted to see "Capernaum-type" miracles, (v.23). Jesus quoted the proverb, *physician heal yourself*, but the Jews did not want to hear his message and so they drove him out of the town and attempted to throw him over a cliff (4:29).

Reflection: *The Lord Jesus, as the great Physician, continues to heal from spiritual blindness. Healing is still administered by the Physician but, as happened at Nazareth, the greatest hindrance can be unbelief.*

JESUS OF NAZARETH

(Acts 2:22)

WE SOMETIMES IDENTIFY PEOPLE by referring to the place where they come from. In the case of Jesus, he had been born in Bethlehem in Judea but had grown up in the small town of Nazareth. Nazareth is not mentioned in the Old Testament and it seems that it was a place of no particular significance.

This was evident when Nathaniel was invited by Philip to come and meet Jesus of Nazareth for he showed his surprise and derision, *Nazareth! Can anything good come from there?* (John 1:46).

After the resurrection of Jesus he revealed himself to Saul on the road to Damascus as *Jesus of Nazareth* (Acts 22:8). Saul had been on a crusade to persecute Christians but now he was faced with the reality of who Jesus really was. Saul at last was ready to acknowledge him as his Lord (Acts 22:8, 10).

Reflection: *What is your estimate of Jesus? Is he only the historical "Jesus of Nazareth" or have you, like Saul, also made him your Lord?*

A MAN ACCREDITED BY GOD

(Acts 2:22)

TO BE "ACCREDITED" MEANS to be qualified or certified for a task. So for Jesus to be accredited by God means that as the Son of God he was sinless and satisfied God's requirements of holiness in order to die and take away the sin of the world.

People had acted in ignorance in crucifying the Lord Jesus, (Acts 3:17), but Peter explained that the crucifixion of Jesus was according to *God's set purpose and foreknowledge* (Acts 2:23).

The people were still responsible for their actions so Peter explained that *God* had *raised this Jesus to life* (Acts 2:32). The resurrection was the ultimate proof that *Jesus of Nazareth* was *the man accredited by God* and so Peter gave the crowd the opportunity to repent (2:38).

Reflection: *The miracles and the resurrection are proof that Jesus was "a man accredited by God". Like the people to whom Peter preached, we too must acknowledge who Jesus is, and through repentance find forgiveness for our sins (Acts 5:31).*

A PRINCE AND SAVIOR
(Acts 5:30, 31)

WHEN THE APOSTLES BEGAN preaching at the Temple many believed and were healed, (Acts 5:12–16), but the outcome resulted in the apostles being arrested and imprisoned (5:16, 17, 26, 27).

The Jewish rulers resented the apostles preaching and making the claim that God had *exalted him (Jesus) to his own right hand as Prince and Savior that he might give repentance and forgiveness of sin to Israel* (5:31).

The title of *Prince* has been variously translated as leader, founder, author and ruler. With this title the Lord Jesus is now exalted to a position of great authority at the right hand of his Father, and as *Savior* he offers *new life* to all who repent and seek his forgiveness (5:20). The Council rejected this message by having the apostles flogged, but the apostles left *rejoicing, because they had been counted worthy of suffering disgrace for the Name,* (5:41).

Reflection: *As "Prince and Savior" the Lord Jesus offers salvation to all who acknowledge his authority as Lord (Romans 10:9).*

LORD AND CHRIST
(Acts 2:36)

AT THE JEWISH FEAST of Pentecost Peter told his listeners that *God had made this Jesus . . . both Lord and Christ* (Messiah). The people were convicted at Peter's message and so he called on them to repent and be baptized, assuring them they would receive forgiveness and the gift of the Holy Spirit, (2:37, 38).

Peter's message is a model of the gospel, for he declared who Jesus was, what he accomplished and the need for repentance. He explained that trusting Jesus for salvation meant acknowledging him as the Messiah and accepting his authority as Lord.

That day around three thousand people believed and were baptized (2:41). What a difference the Holy Spirit made to Peter's preaching and this was only the beginning of the new Church in action.

Reflection: *God made him to be both "Lord and Christ". As the Christ, he was God's anointed servant fulfilling God's purposes on earth. As our Savior he has the right to be our Lord, for he is both "Lord and Christ".*

THE HOLY AND RIGHTEOUS ONE

(Acts 3:14)

THE CROWD WOULD HAVE been surprised to hear Peter refer to the Lord Jesus by the title *the Holy and Righteous One*, for *the Holy One* (Psalm 22:3) and *the Righteous One* (Isaiah 24:16) were Old Testament titles for God. They would have known that God's holiness was descriptive of his character through which he displayed his perfection and his essential goodness in both blessing and judging his people.

The evidence of his holiness was seen in his righteousness, because all that he did was in perfect harmony with his character. As Isaiah had said, *the LORD Almighty will be exalted by his justice, and the holy God will show himself holy by his righteousness* (Isaiah 5:16).

The implication of Peter's message was clear to his listeners. The *Holy and Righteous One* was none other than the Messiah they crucified. Shocked by what they heard many of his listeners now believed (Acts 4:4).

Reflection: *Today others should see in us evidence of God's holiness and his righteousness.*

THE AUTHOR OF LIFE

(Acts 3:15)

WHILE PREACHING AT THE Temple Peter accused his audience of being responsible for the death of Jesus. *You killed the author of life*, he said.

This title indicates that Peter understood that life originated with our Lord who was with the Father at creation. The Apostle John confirms this truth when he writes, *through him all things were made, without him nothing was made that has been made* (John 1:3).

Therefore, from heaven's glory Jesus came to earth to become the *author of life* by giving himself *for the life of the world* (John 6:51). It was the Father's will *that everyone who looks to the Son and believes in him shall have eternal life* (6:40).

Reflection: *Today we have the assurance that our names are written in the "book of life" (Revelation 3:5). Therefore we honor the "author of life" by our lives and through our worship, for he "destroyed death and has brought life and immortality to light through the gospel" (2 Timothy 1:10).*

THE ANOINTED ONE
(Acts 4:26)

IN THE NEW TESTAMENT, the title *the Anointed One* is equivalent to the titles, *the Christ, the Chosen One* and *the Messiah*. So, as God's *Anointed One,* Jesus was chosen by God as the One who would come to the help of his people.

Peter not only recognized Jesus as the *Anointed One* (Acts 4:26) but he understood that Jesus had an anointing on his life, for he said *God anointed Jesus of Nazareth with the Holy Spirit and power* (Acts 10:38). Jesus also spoke about this anointing when he said, *The Spirit of the Lord is on me and has anointed me to preach the gospel* (Luke 4:18).

The New Testament believers were no longer given an anointing with oil to set them apart for God's service as happened in the Old Testament, but like the Lord Jesus, we today *have an anointing from the Holy Spirit* (1 John 2:20–27).

Reflection: *This anointing should mean power for living a holy life that is characterized by love in our service.*

THE MAN HE HAS APPOINTED
(Acts 17:31)

ON PAUL'S SECOND MISSIONARY journey he visited Athens speaking to a group of philosophers who had authority in their city over religion and morals. It was Paul's first occasion to explain the gospel to a group who had no understanding of the Jewish Old Testament. In Luke's summary of Paul's message he alludes to the resurrection of Jesus as *the man he* (God) *has appointed* who will one day *judge the world.*

The mention of Christ's resurrection started a debate where it was probably difficult for Paul to continue preaching. Some sneered at the idea of a resurrection and a judgement but others believed, (17:32–34).

Jesus himself had earlier recognized his future role when he said, *the Father judges no one, but has entrusted all judgment to the Son* (John 5:22).

Reflection: *The knowledge that everyone "must appear before the judgment seat of Christ" (2 Corinthians 5:10), and "give account . . . for every careless word they have spoken" (Matthew 12:36); should be a powerful incentive to holy living.*

CHRIST, WHO IS GOD OVER ALL
(Romans 9:5)

IN 2 KINGS 19:15 we are told that the *God of Israel* was *God over all the kingdoms of the earth* and it was Paul's point that, as *God over all,* he had the right to choose whom he would bless, (Romans 9).

Now in a discussion about God's choice to build the nation of Israel, Paul established God's right to also extend his mercy to the Gentile nations. Israel did not attain righteousness because their attempts to achieve it were through their own efforts (9:31, 32). Now in Christ a remnant of Jews will be saved (9:27) along with the Gentiles who obtain their righteousness through faith (9:30).

In view of what Christ accomplished for us, Paul's response was to worship *Christ, who is God over all, forever praised! Amen.*

Reflection: *We who were the "objects of his wrath" have now become the "objects of his mercy" (9:22, 23). We too like Paul should say "Amen" and worship the "Christ, who is God over all".*

JESUS IS LORD
(Romans 10:9)

THE NAME *JESUS* COMES from the Hebrew name Joshua meaning, "the LORD is salvation", so the title *Jesus is Lord* acknowledges his authority in our lives as our Master. To *believe in* Jesus as our Savior therefore means we must also *confess* him as Lord, (Romans 10:9).

The words *believe* and *confess* refer to our response to *Jesus as Lord*. To *believe* is to accept, to trust and to depend on Jesus for our salvation. To *confess* is to give expression to our faith by acknowledging or demonstrating it to others.

Paul balanced belief and confession by saying that belief establishes us in a right relationship with God, while confession complements our belief and completes our salvation (10:10). The title *Jesus is Lord* was perhaps the earliest statement by Christians to indicate their common faith in Jesus.

Reflection: *To declare that "Jesus is Lord" is to speak powerfully to the world and to the principalities and powers (Ephesians 6:12). We demonstrate his Lordship by our obedience and our confession.*

THE LORD OF ALL
(Romans 10:12–13)

IN ROMANS 10, PAUL introduced this title for Jesus when he demonstrated that Jesus was Lord of all by making his righteousness available for everyone who believes (10:4, 12). The word "everyone" applies to both Jews and Gentiles (10:12) for the distinguishing characteristic of God's people is no longer on the basis of race but on faith in Christ.

The words believe (10:10), trusts (10:11), call on his name (10:12) and faith (10:17) are all used to describe the response that people need to make for the salvation and the blessing he offers.

When we consider that there is an unseen world of evil, we can also be thankful for the salvation and blessing of the Lord to keep us safe in our struggle against the powers of this dark world (Ephesians 6:12).

Reflection: *Jesus Christ is "Lord of all and richly blesses those who call on him". Thank him for the blessing of his salvation and his ongoing power to keep and protect you.*

A DELIVERER
(Romans 11:26)

THE TITLE "DELIVERER" OCCURS once in Romans 11 where it is quoted from Isaiah 59:20. Paul has borrowed the metaphor of an olive tree from Jeremiah 11:16, and likened the tree to the people of Israel. The original tree has had some of its unbelieving Jewish branches removed.

As Gentile people have believed the gospel they, like a *wild olive shoot,* have been grafted into the tree (Romans 11:17). There is a balance in Paul's writing in this chapter between Israel's responsibility not to *persist in unbelief* and the promise made by the *Deliverer* to turn *godlessness from Jacob* (Israel) (11:26).

Paul's message comes with a warning to all Christians to *consider therefore the kindness and sternness of God, sternness to those who fell, but kindness to you, provided that you continue in his kindness. Otherwise you also will be cut off* (11:22).

Reflection: *Paul has used the example of what happened to some in Israel, as a warning to us all.*

THE LORD OF BOTH THE DEAD AND THE LIVING
(Romans 14:9)

WE USUALLY THINK OF Christ's death and resurrection in terms of the salvation he provides for all those who believe, but the verse above puts salvation in a broader context. Paul says, *it was for this very reason that Christ died . . . that he might be Lord of both the dead and the living.*

Earlier in the chapter Paul had dealt with two problems facing the Church at Rome. There was the matter of eating meat (14:3) and the matter of keeping special days as holy (14:5).

These matters may not be an issue for us today, but the principles that Paul established are important. Such matters Paul says are for private interpretation and should not be a barrier to fellowship in the Church.

Reflection: *For Jesus to be "Lord of both the dead and the living" is a reminder that there is no escape from his authority and his judgment, for we must all give an account of our lives to God.*

A SERVANT OF THE JEWS
(Romans 15:8, 9)

GOD'S CHOSEN PEOPLE WERE called "Israel" after the name God had given Jacob (Genesis 32:28), but later they were also called Jews after Judah, one of Jacob's sons. When Paul referred to Jesus as a *servant of the Jews,* he was acknowledging that Jesus had focused his work mainly on teaching the Jewish people.

In Romans 15:8, 9 Paul explains that Jesus' coming was to *confirm the promises made to the patriarchs,* who were the early fathers of the Jewish nation. God had made his covenant promises with them to bless their descendants (Genesis 17:7).

But these covenant promises had also made reference to the blessings that would flow to other nations. For instance, God had said to Abraham, *through your offspring all nations on earth will be blessed* (Genesis 22:18).

Reflection: *The blessing to "all nations" has come to us through the message of the gospel. Make sure you play your part in praying, supporting and advancing the cause of the gospel.*

NAMES FOR, AND REFERENCES TO, GOD THE SON, OUR LORD JESUS CHRIST

CHRIST THE POWER OF GOD
(1 Corinthians 1:24)

PAUL VIEWED THE CREATION as evidence of God's power, for he wrote, *since the creation of the world God's invisible qualities . . . his eternal power and divine nature . . . have been clearly seen* (Romans 1:20). For Israel, God's power was evident in his protection of them as a nation, in their release from slavery in Egypt and from their captivity in Babylon.

In the New Testament Paul also saw the good news about Christ's death and resurrection as evidence of God's power. He wrote to the Christians at Rome. *I am not ashamed of the gospel, because it is the power of God for the salvation of everyone who believes* (Romans 1:16).

Whereas in the Old Testament God's power was evident in his creation and in the deliverance of Israel, now *Christ the power of* God brings spiritual deliverance to his people through their salvation.

Reflection: *Our strength to love others, to live a holy life and to serve him must come from "Christ the power of God".*

CHRIST . . . THE WISDOM OF GOD
(1 Corinthians 1:24)

"WISDOM" CAN BE DEFINED as true knowledge combined with sound judgment that leads to prudent action. In Paul's time however, Greek culture equated wisdom with philosophy and their sophists or teachers who were skilled in argument and debate were considered to be wise.

In the first two chapters of 1 Corinthians Paul discussed the nature of true wisdom and mentioned the word thirteen times in these chapters as he exposed human wisdom as foolishness.

God in his wisdom sent his Son to give his life in order to bring salvation to the world. This was Paul's message but many Jews could not understand it, and the Gentiles thought it was foolishness (1:22, 23).

Reflection: *With Christ as our head, we are his Church and demonstrate "the manifold wisdom of God to the spiritual powers of the unseen world" (Ephesians 3:10). In the same way as a gemstone reflects the light and makes it sparkle, so God's wisdom in all its variety and glory should be seen shining through God's people.*

OUR RIGHTEOUSNESS, HOLINESS, AND REDEMPTION
(1 Corinthians 1:30)

CHRIST IN DYING FOR us demonstrated God's wisdom so that his *righteousness, holiness and redemption* should be made available to us. *Righteousness* and *holiness* are attributes of God's character and come to us from the wisdom of God through our redemption in Christ.

As our righteousness, Christ has made us righteous through faith in him for salvation. Paul called this *a righteousness that comes by faith* (Romans 4:13).

As our holiness, the writer to the Hebrews refers to Christ as *the one who makes men holy* (2:11), for he has set us apart from the world as his holy people and by his Spirit continues to develop the holiness of his character within us.

As our redemption, Christ *gave himself for us to redeem us from all wickedness,* (Titus 2:14).

Reflection: *Of the many world religions it is only Christ who offers salvation as a free gift. This is because "Christ has become for us wisdom from God–that is, our righteousness, holiness and redemption."*

CHRIST OUR PASSOVER LAMB
(1 Corinthians 5:7)

THE ORIGINAL OLD TESTAMENT Passover meal was first celebrated by the Israelites on the night prior to their deliverance by God from slavery in Egypt. Each family took the blood of an unblemished lamb or goat and sprinkled some of it on the surrounding doorframe of the house and then roasted the animal for an evening celebration meal.

That night the angel of death "passed over" the houses killing the first born of men and animals in places where there was no blood on the door posts (Exodus 12).

Paul reflected on this Jewish Passover feast and referred to the sacrifice of the Lord Jesus as *our Passover*. To have our sins covered by Christ's blood means that we have his cleansing and protection, as God's judgment of sin has "passed over" and has not come to us.

Reflection: *Since "Christ our Passover Lamb has been sacrificed" we are to "keep the festival" of Communion as a celebration in remembrance of his death for us.*

THE LORD OF GLORY

(1 Corinthians 2:8)

IN THE VERSE ABOVE, Paul said that had the rulers of the nation understood who Jesus really was, they would not have crucified the Lord of glory. "Glory" refers to the majesty, beauty and honor associated with the presence and the ministry of the Lord Jesus, so we can see why Paul referred to Jesus as the Lord of glory, for all glory belongs to him.

John also spoke about the Lord's glory saying that Jesus had come to earth from sharing the glory he had with his Father, (John 17:5), and that the disciples had seen his glory (1:14).

Jesus had viewed his ministry of healing as being for God's glory and in bringing life to Lazarus, he too would be glorified (John 11:4).

Reflection: *Since we now enjoy the presence of the "Spirit of Glory" (1 Peter 4:14), we can understand Paul's concern that God's people should be diligent in their service, "for this is to my Father's glory that you bear much fruit (John 15:8).*

THE ROCK

(1 Corinthians 10:4)

A Stumbling Stone (Romans 9:32)

IN THE OLD TESTAMENT God is referred to as a *Rock* as he was a source of deliverance, protection and blessing for Israel.

However, in the New Testament the image of Christ as a *Rock* brings a warning (1 Corinthians 10:1–13). The Israelites had drunk water from a rock that was a symbol of Christ's spiritual presence accompanying them—*and that rock was Christ*. The Israelites, however, sinned repeatedly and most died before reaching their promised land.

In Romans 9:30–33, there is the warning for the Jews who did not believe in Jesus. He was to them *a stumbling stone . . . a rock that makes them fall* (9:32, 33). Then thirdly there is a warning in the parable about building on a foundation of sand rather than rock which is a reference again to Jesus (Matthew.7:24–27).

Reflection: *In these references to Jesus as a rock there is the warning that people will attempt to build their lives on a foundation other than Christ the Rock.*

THE FIRST FRUITS

(1 Corinthians 15:20)

AT THE BEGINNING OF the barley harvest the Jewish people held the feast of *Unleavened Bread*. It was a week-long festival that started with the Passover meal celebrating their exodus from slavery in Egypt.

The following day the *first fruits* of the harvest in the form of a sheaf of barley were waved before the Lord as an offering. The grain was then roasted and then ground into flour and burnt along with an animal sacrifice (Leviticus 23:9–11). The offering was a reminder that God had given to them their land and therefore they could celebrate the coming harvest.

For the resurrection of Christ to be referred to as the *first fruits of those who have fallen asleep* is an assurance of a future resurrection of God's people when we will one day join our Lord in the glory.

Reflection: *The "first fruits" offering of our Lord gives us hope of a life to come. We therefore have a wonderful future to look forward to, for which we should give thanks.*

THE LAST ADAM

(1 Corinthians 15:45)

ADAM AND EVE SINNED against God when they ate of the forbidden fruit and were then expelled from the Garden of Eden (Genesis 3). The serious consequence of their disobedience was the entry of sin into God's perfect creation.

Paul contrasted the failure of Adam with the achievement of Jesus Christ when he compared our spiritual death in Adam with our spiritual life in Christ. *For as in Adam all die, so in Christ all will be made alive,* (1 Corinthians 15:22).

The difference between what Adam and Christ did is highlighted even further by the contrast of the two names, *the first Adam* and *the last Adam*. *The first Adam became a living being, the last Adam a life giving Spirit* (15:45).

Reflection: *What Adam destroyed and what Christ restored are the two events that have dominated and shaped the course of human history. As descendants of Adam we were born sinners (Psalm 51:5); but in Christ we have been born again, (1 Peter 1:23).*

NAMES FOR, AND REFERENCES TO, GOD THE SON, OUR LORD JESUS CHRIST

THE MAN FROM HEAVEN
(1 Corinthians 15:49)

IN 1 CORINTHIANS 15:21; 45–47, and in Romans 5:15–19, Paul compares Adam, the first man and the Lord Jesus, *the man from heaven.*

The first contrast is between death and resurrection. *For since death came through a man, the resurrection of the dead comes also through a man* (1 Corinthians.15:21). Paul then developed this contrast when he said, *the first Adam became a living being, the last Adam a life-giving spirit . . . The first man was of the dust of the earth, the second man from heaven* (15:45, 47).

In Romans 5:12–20, the contrast is between a reign of death and a reign in life. The outcome of the trespass is that *death reigned from the time of Adam,* had universal application (5:14) and brought judgment and condemnation (5:16). By contrast, the gift of God (5:15) was the Lord Jesus himself, *a gift of righteousness* which brought a reign in life (5:17), his eternal life (5:21).

Reflection: *What an accomplishment by the "man from heaven" bringing us eternal life.*

JESUS CHRIST IS LORD
(Philippians 2:11)

IN OLD TESTAMENT TIMES Jewish people occasionally had to sell themselves as slaves in order to pay their debts, but under Jewish law they had to be set free after serving a period of not more than six years. Sometimes, however, a slave grew to love his master and preferred to continue serving him rather than gain his freedom.

In this event, the master would drill a hole in the lobe of the servant's ear and thus the servant would become a "bond-slave" for life (Deuteronomy 15:12–18). To this slave his pierced ear-lobe was like a badge of honor declaring publicly his lifetime commitment to his master.

For us today slavery carries unpleasant connotations of enforced labor, loss of personal freedom and dignity, and a relationship in which people are exploited.

Reflection: *Paul developed the idea of a master/slave relationship calling himself a "bond-slave" of Jesus Christ (1 Corinthians 9:19, RSV). He acknowledged that one day everybody "will confess that Jesus Christ is Lord" (Philippians 2:11).*

A HUSBAND
(2 Corinthians 11:2)

In the same way as the Old Testament portrayed God as the "husband" of Israel (Hosea 2:16), so the wife/husband relationship is used by Paul to picture the Church in relation to Christ.

As their spiritual father who first introduced them to faith in Christ, he likened himself to a father arranging the marriage of his daughter. Having promised his daughter in marriage, the father would be anxious that she kept herself pure until she was presented to her husband on the wedding day.

Paul is using the strongest imagery to urge the Christians at Corinth to see themselves as a bride waiting with expectation for the arrival of the bridegroom, their husband. They must therefore prepare for this grand occasion and keep themselves pure in their faith.

Reflection: *With our Lord Jesus as our "Husband" there is a clear warning against spiritual adultery. Like Corinth, we too live within a godless culture which will lead us astray from our devotion to Christ (2 Corinthians 11:3).*

HIS INDESCRIBABLE GIFT
(2 Corinthians 9:15)

God has given to the world the indescribable gift of his Son. No one can pay God for his gift as it can only be accepted or refused.

The above reference is the only place in the Bible where something is described as indescribable, so God's gift is unique and there is nothing to which it can be compared. Paul states that the gift of God is eternal life, (Romans 6:23), so for us to receive the indescribable gift of God's Son, means that we accept Christ as our Savior and Lord who gives us his eternal life.

Further, receiving God's *indescribable gift* means that we also receive his *gift* of the Holy Spirit to live within us (Acts 10:45). The presence of the Holy Spirit means that he develops the character of Christ in us and equips us with his gifts so that we can serve our Lord effectively.

Reflection: *Remember to be thankful to God for the "indescribable gift" of his Son.*

THE ONE HE LOVES
(Ephesians 1:5, 6)

In Paul's day, if a Roman family had no sons the parents might adopt a boy in order to ensure the continuation of the family name. The father of this family had absolute authority over his children and when a son was adopted the courts regarded him as a new person.

Any former debts were cancelled and his former father lost all influence over him. The adopted son began a new life with new privileges and responsibilities under the authority of his new father. Paul wants us to keep this background in mind when he says that God has chosen us and adopted us into his family through *the One he loves*—our Lord Jesus.

We are therefore released from the control of Satan, our debt of sin has been forgiven and Satan no longer has any authority over us.

Reflection: *We now have the privileges and responsibilities of belonging to a new Father in the family of God, adopted by "the One He Loves".*

YOUR SEED
(Genesis 3:15, Galatians 3:16)

The above verse from Genesis is the first prophetic reference in the Bible to the future Messiah and provides a glimpse into the hostility he would experience in coming to earth as the *seed* or offspring of Eve.

Messiah would triumph over Satan, for Messiah *will crush your head*. However, in order to bring salvation to men and women, he would have to suffer Satan's attack, for Satan would *strike his heel*.

Paul referred to the Genesis verse above when he wrote to the Galatians and argued that the term "seed", which is a collective noun, can also be used in the singular. Paul explained that it is the singular use of the word that refers to the one seed *who is Christ,* who crushed Satan's head.

Reflection: *Have you ever wondered why there is such hostility in the world against the Jews and Christians? The problem goes back to the sin of Adam and Eve and the hostility towards God's people from those in Satan's dominion of darkness.*

THE HEAD THAT IS CHRIST
(Ephesians 4:15)

PAUL LIKENED THE RELATIONSHIP between Christ and the Church to the functioning of a human body. In the same way as a human body is controlled by its head, so the Church is to be controlled by its *Head that is Christ*.

People are responsible for conducting the activities of the Church, but it is always a delegated responsibility under the authority of *the Head*.

Further, members of the Church have to *grow up into him who is the Head*. "Growing up" means functioning in the body of Christ in harmony with others so that the gifts which we have are used to bless others and bring glory to *the head, that is Christ* (Ephesians 4:15, 16). Paul warned the Colossians that their false teachers had *lost connection with the Head* (2:19). What a warning!

Reflection: *Only the experience of a living relationship with Jesus Christ based on the truth of His Word and loving relationships with others will ensure "connection with the Head".*

OUR PEACE
(Ephesians 2:14, 15)

IN THESE VERSES THE Lord Jesus is spoken of as *our peace* as he had died to take away the sin of the world. This work, in reconciling Jews and Gentiles to God and to each other, is described as *destroying the barrier, the wall of hostility*.

Within the Temple area at Jerusalem there was a stone wall separating the Temple building from the outer area called the "Court of the Gentiles". Non-Jews were forbidden to go beyond this wall. This *dividing wall* was possibly in Paul's thinking when he wrote the above verses.

The *law with its commandments and regulations* kept the Jewish people bound to their animal sacrifices and belief system where they considered themselves to be righteous. Thus these regulations were a *wall of hostility* which had now been destroyed through Christ's death.

Reflection: *Our world is still divided by race, political ideology, cultural differences and religion, but Christ's "purpose was to create in himself one new man out of the two, thus making peace" (Ephesians 2:15b).*

A FRAGRANT OFFERING AND SACRIFICE

Live a life of love, just as Christ loved us and gave himself up for us as a fragrant offering and sacrifice to God, (Ephesians 5:2).

THIS LANGUAGE OF "FRAGRANCE" and "sacrifice" used in connection with worship refers to the Old Testament sacrificial system.

Fragrance was made through mixing certain gums and resins and was used in worship at the Tabernacle (Exodus 30:34–38). The fragrance was placed in front of the Ark of the Covenant within the Holy Place and was also added to some of the burnt offerings. We read that such offerings had *an aroma pleasing to the LORD* (Leviticus 2:2).

But the sacrifice of Christ on the cross required no added incense to make it pleasing to God. As the perfect and final atonement for sin, God accepted Christ's sacrifice of himself for us, *as a fragrant offering and sacrifice.*

Reflection: *For us to "live a life of love" means that our lives too will be a fragrant offering acceptable to God.*

THE CARPENTER, MARY'S SON

"What's this wisdom that has been given him that he even does miracles! Isn't this the carpenter? Isn't this Mary's son?
(Mark 6:2, 3)

ON THE OCCASION JESUS arrived back to his home-town of Nazareth the local people were interested to hear what he had to say at their Synagogue service. They knew about his miracles at Capernaum, but when he commented on the Scriptures people were surprised at his knowledge and understanding.

For people who knew him as *the Carpenter, Mary's son,* with brothers and sisters living nearby, their reaction to Jesus revealed their jealousy and so *they took offense at him.* The people did not understand who Jesus really was and their failure to trust him meant that Jesus was limited in what he could do to help them (6:5–6).

Reflection: *We will also limit God by our unbelief, but if we trust in the Lord and expect him to work through his Holy Spirit, then things can be different. Pray and prepare to be surprised.*

THE IMAGE OF THE INVISIBLE GOD
(Colossians 1:15)

PAUL SAID OF JESUS, *Who being in very nature God . . . being made in human likeness and being found in appearance as a man, he humbled himself* (Philippians 2:7, 8).

With the nature of God, Jesus lived on earth as the God/Man. As a man, Jesus was *the exact representation* of his Father, (Hebrews 1:3). So, as *the image of the invisible God* he lived on earth in the *likeness* of man, (Philippians 2:7).

There is a difference between these words "image" and "likeness". As *the image of God* Jesus was the perfect representation of his Father. But Jesus could never be the perfect representation of sinful man. Therefore Scripture makes the distinction. He came to earth as *the image of God* but in *the likeness of man.*

Reflection: *Men and women were created in the image of God (Genesis 1:27), but through sin that image was defaced. Now God's people are again being "renewed in knowledge in the image of its Creator" (Colossians 3:10). What a change!*

THE BEGINNING AND THE FIRST BORN FROM AMONG THE DEAD
(Colossians 1:18)

AS "THE BEGINNING," THE Lord Jesus brought the creation into being. *Through him all things were made* (John 1:3). He was also *the beginning* of a new spiritual creation offering eternal life, (2 Corinthians 5:17). This eternal life was *promised before the beginning of time* (Titus 1:2).

The title, "the first born from the dead", expands this *beginning* title for the Lord Jesus was the first to enjoy a resurrection life. People such as Lazarus (John 11) and the widow's son from Nain (Luke 7:11–15) were also raised from death but being mortals they later died.

The Lord Jesus alone rose from the dead never to die again, for he *destroyed death and has brought life and immortality to light through the gospel* (2 Timothy 1:10).

Reflection: *We too will one day enjoy a resurrection from death. Then "our mortality will give way to immortality" as we enter the presence of our Lord (1 Corinthians 15:53, 54). This indeed is a cause to rejoice.*

THE HOPE OF GLORY
(Colossians 1:27)

WE OFTEN USE THE word "hope" to express an uncertain wish. For instance, we might say, "I hope it won't rain". Such a hope lacks certainty especially if rain has been forecast.

In contrast, the Bible uses the word "hope" to refer to something certain. Therefore, Christ's presence in our lives as *the hope of glory* means that he gives us the assurance of a future glorious inheritance.

Paul wrote similarly of *God our Savior* and of *Christ Jesus our hope* (1 Timothy 1:1). It was God who made his plan of redemption known to the Gentile nations through Christ. It is through Christ our *hope of glory* that our redemption will be realized as we go to be with him.

Reflection: *The blessing of Christ's presence in our lives, bringing hope of a glorious eternal future, was the mystery revealed to the world through Christ's coming. Having this understanding should motivate us towards giving priority to living life in a way that pleases our Lord.*

THE HEAD OVER EVERY POWER AND AUTHORITY
(Colossians 2:10)

THESE POWERS AND AUTHORITIES refer to people and governments as well as supernatural angels and demons that influence the affairs of this world. They are nevertheless subject to our Lord as *Head over every power and authority*.

We live our lives therefore, in the presence of spiritual beings, but for God's people we have the presence of his Holy Spirit living within us to guide and strengthen us.

The day is coming when our Lord *will hand over the kingdom to God the Father after he has destroyed all dominion, authority and power* (1 Corinthians 15:24, 25). In the meantime, Paul says that we must *struggle . . . against the rulers, against the authorities, against the powers of this dark world and against the spiritual forces of evil in the heavenly realms* (Ephesians 6:12).

Reflection: *Our prayers, our witness and our service for the Lord are all weapons in this struggle, and victory is ours, for "I can do everything through him who gives me strength" (Philippians 4:13).*

A MASTER IN HEAVEN
(Colossians 3:24; 4:1)

THE MANUAL WORKERS OF the Roman Empire were its slaves and many Christians in the New Testament Churches were either slaves or people who owned slaves. If slaves ran away and were later recaptured they could be either killed or branded on the forehead with the letter "F" for *fugitivus*, meaning a runaway or fugitive.

It is interesting to note that Paul's letter to the Church at Colosse was to be carried by Tychicus and the slave Onesimus (4:7–9) who was "a runaway". Onesimus had now become a Christian and Paul was sending him back to Colosse to his Christian master Philemon, asking him to accept him back as a Christian brother (Philemon 9–17).

Slaves by law were not allowed to own anything, so it must have been a source of encouragement for them to know that they had an inheritance in heaven to look forward to (Colossians 3:24).

Reflection: *As "bond slaves" to our "Master in Heaven" remember that we too have an inheritance to look forward to.*

OUR LORD JESUS CHRIST
(1 Thessalonians 1:3)

PAUL HAD VISITED THESSALONICA on his second missionary journey for only a short stay, but some Jews and many Greeks had responded to the gospel, (Acts 17:4). Now in writing to the Church, his opening greeting is a reminder that they are in *God the Father and the Lord Jesus Christ* (1:1).

Eleven times in his two letters to the Thessalonians Paul used this name that encompasses so much of who Jesus is. As the "Christ" or Messiah he fulfilled Old Testament prophecies as the Lord's Anointed One who would redeem his people. The name "Jesus" had been given to him at his birth by the angel (Matthew 1:21). The name comes from the Hebrew meaning Joshua, "the Lord is Salvation".

But for Christians, he was above all their "Lord", a name that indicated his deity as well as being their Master who should be worshipped and obeyed.

Reflection: *Jesus Christ died and rose again that he might be Lord (Romans 14:9).*

THE LORD OF PEACE
(2 Thessalonians 3:16)

IN THE NEW TESTAMENT it is the Lord Jesus who is *the Lord of peace* and his presence with us is our source of peace, because we are reconciled to him through his death, (Ephesians 2:16). The word "reconciled" means that a peaceful relationship with God has been restored to us.

Jesus warned his disciples that they could expect to be persecuted (John 15:20), and to have troubles (John 16:33). Jesus would not remove them from difficult situations but he would give them his peace so that they did not need to be troubled or afraid (John 14:27).

It is also the work of the Holy Spirit in us to produce this quality of peace (Galatians 5:22). Enjoying his peace gives us a sense of well-being and contentment in our lives which should help us to face the stress of living in a busy world.

Reflection: *Now "the Lord of peace himself will give you peace." Have you ever thought of yourself as a peacemaker?*

CHRIST JESUS OUR HOPE
(1 Timothy 1:1)

IN THE OLD TESTAMENT God is called the *Hope of Israel* (Jeremiah 14:8, 17:13). In the New Testament, "hope" is a title that refers to both *the God of hope* (Romans 15:13) and to *Christ Jesus our hope* (1 Timothy 1:1).

Because it *was God who reconciled us to himself through Christ* (2 Corinthians 5:19), the Lord Jesus is the object of our hope and gives to us the assurance of a secure future.

The hope of eternal life was promised before the beginning of time, (Titus 1:2). This eternal life is nothing less than the life of Christ that we share now and look forward to sharing with him in the future. In the meantime we are told to wait *for the blessed hope . . . the glorious appearing of our great God and Savior Jesus Christ.*

Reflection: *"Christ in you the hope of glory" (Colossians 1:27). What a hope to look forward to, a "hope that is stored up for us in heaven" (Colossians 1:5).*

THE MAN CHRIST JESUS
(1 Timothy 2:5)

THE TITLE, "THE MAN Christ Jesus", emphasizes the humanity of our Lord and his anointed purpose in being sent by God the Father to carry out his will in becoming *the Savior of the world,* (1 John 4:14).

As the only sinless man who ever lived, he alone qualified to become a *ransom for all men* in order to satisfy the requirements of a holy God. The death of the *man Christ Jesus* demonstrated that *God our Savior wants all men to be saved and to come to a knowledge of the truth* (1 Timothy 2:4).

For sinful men and women to be reconciled to a holy God there had to be someone who could represent them to God. Men and women could only take the punishment for their own sin. Therefore *God our Savior* had to send his Son to earth as *the man Christ Jesus.*

Reflection: *There is only one God, and one way to God, that is through the man Christ Jesus.*

THE MASTER

In a large house there are articles not only of gold and silver, but also of wood and clay; some are for noble purposes and some for ignoble. If a man cleanses himself from the latter he will be an instrument for noble purposes, made holy, useful to the Master and prepared to do any good work, (2 Timothy 2:20, 21).

IN THESE VERSES PAUL likened God's people to these household articles. He emphasized that to be *useful to the Master*—the Lord Jesus, and to be used *for noble* or honorable *purposes,* we need to be cleansed from anything that would defile us.

The Greek word that Paul used for *Master* is "despotes" from which we get the English word "despot" meaning a ruler with absolute authority. Paul used this strong word for Master to heighten the contrast between the unlimited power and authority of *the Master* with the lowly position of us as *instruments.*

Reflection: *What a privilege it is being used in God's household by the Master for his noble purposes.*

NAMES FOR, AND REFERENCES TO, GOD THE SON, OUR LORD JESUS CHRIST

OUR GREAT GOD AND SAVIOR JESUS CHRIST
(Titus 2:13)

PAUL IN THIS VERSE and Peter in his greeting in 2 Peter 1:1, use this name emphasizing the deity of Jesus as truly God. Paul in writing to Titus refers to the greatness of our God and Savior in a context where he encouraged him to stress to his listeners a holiness of lifestyle.

He said, we need *to live self-controlled, upright and godly lives in this present age, while we wait for the blessed hope—the glorious appearing of our great God and Savior, Jesus Christ* (Titus 2:12, 13).

The knowledge that *our great God and Savior Jesus Christ* has given us a faith (2 Peter 1:1), and is one day coming back for his Church, is both a *blessed hope* that we look forward to, and an incentive to order our lives as we prepare to meet him.

Reflection: *To know our Lord as "our Great God and Savior Jesus Christ" is to understand more fully the One who died as our Savior.*

THE HEIR OF ALL THINGS

In these last days he has spoken to us by his Son, whom he appointed heir of all things, (Hebrews 1:2).

IT IS THE USUAL practice in most cultures for the children in a family to be the heirs to the inheritance of their parents. On occasions, only male offspring were entitled to the inheritance and sometimes it was the elder son who benefitted. The right to an inheritance is always a privilege conveyed by people to those they love.

For the writer of the Hebrews to record that the Lord Jesus was *appointed heir of all things,* indicated that the Son not only enjoyed the Father's favor, but satisfied his purpose for creation. Thus God speaks to us through his Son who is supreme over all.

Reflection: *We too have an inheritance to look forward to. "If we are children then we are heirs–heirs of God and co-heirs with Christ" (Romans 8:17). It is amazing to know God regards us as his "glorious inheritance" (Ephesians 1:18).*

THE RADIANCE OF GOD'S GLORY
(Hebrews 1:3)

A CENTRAL TRUTH IN the book of Hebrews is that Jesus Christ has perfectly revealed God the Father to the world. This truth is expressed in the metaphor that the *Son is the radiance of God's glory*. In the same way as the sun reveals its glory through the sunlight, so the Son of God is the *radiance* or brightness *of God's glory* to us.

At the outset of Jesus' ministry, John recorded that they had *seen his glory, the glory of the One and Only* (John 1:14). To unbelievers, who failed to see him as the *radiance of God's glory*, he was just a man, the carpenter's son.

Today *the radiance of God's glory* is evident in the lives of believers through the presence of the *Spirit of glory* (1 Peter 4:14). His glory in us is revealed as we grow in likeness to our Lord (2 Corinthians 3:18).

Reflection: *A Prayer: "Lord, help me to reflect your glory as I seek to live for you today".*

THE EXACT REPRESENTATION OF HIS BEING
(Hebrews 1:3)

AS THE RADIANCE OF *God's glory*, the Lord Jesus reveals the majesty of God to men and women, but he can only do this because he is *the exact representation of his being*.

The words "*exact representation*" are translated from the one Greek word and convey the idea of a perfect copy of an original. In the same way as a coin is stamped from a die so that the impression on the new coin is identical in form to the die itself, so Jesus as a man expressed perfectly the person and character of his Father.

Through this title the writer declared the deity of Jesus as the God/Man. He was able to live in such close communion with, and dependence on, his Father because he was the *exact representation of his being*.

Reflection: *As a member of the family of God you too share the family likeness and should seek to faithfully represent him.*

THE ONE WHO MAKES MEN HOLY

Both the one who makes men holy and those who are made holy are of the same family. So Jesus is not ashamed to call them brothers, (Hebrews 2:11).

THE WORDS "MADE HOLY" in the verse above explain what the Lord Jesus has done in the life of every believer. Holiness means a purity of life based on Christ's work of redemption in which he restored us to a relationship with our heavenly Father. *We have been made holy through the sacrifice of the body of Jesus Christ once for all* (Hebrews 10:10).

Holiness is also an ongoing process in which we separate ourselves from sin and the Spirit of God develops the character of Christ in our lives, changing us into his likeness (2 Corinthians 3:18). In this sense *we are being made holy.* (Hebrews 10:14).

Reflection: *It is mind boggling to think that we belong to the same family as Jesus our Lord, and that he is not ashamed to call us his brothers (2:11).*

THE APOSTLE AND HIGH PRIEST
(Hebrews 3:1)

AN APOSTLE IS AN envoy or messenger who is sent with authority to represent another person or institution. For Jesus to be *the Apostle,* means that he was sent to earth from his Father in heaven with the specific task of revealing his Father to his followers and of teaching them about his Kingdom.

The title of *high priest* refers to the work the Lord Jesus did in order to save his people. Whereas the Old Testament sacrifices had to be repeated, *Jesus the high priest* had to offer himself only once as the *atoning sacrifice for our sins* (1 John 2:2).

Further, he returned to heaven where as our high priest *he always lives to intercede* for us (Hebrews 7:25). These two titles therefore capture what our Lord accomplished for us.

Reflection: *The writer says that "we should consider carefully Jesus the apostle and high priest whom we confess". The nature of our confession will depend on our consideration of Jesus as our "apostle and high priest".*

THE SOURCE OF ETERNAL SALVATION

Although he was a son, he learned obedience from what he suffered and, once made perfect, he became the source of eternal salvation for all who obey him (Hebrews 5:8, 9).

JESUS HAD COME TO earth in obedience to the will of his Father, as it was only on earth that he could experience human suffering and resist Satan's temptations. Thus he had a complete experience of manhood and demonstrated his perfect obedience to the will of his Father.

The writer of the Hebrews referred to this earthly experience of Jesus as one in which he *learned obedience from what he suffered.*

By enduring the humiliation and rejection of men and by his death for us on the cross he was *made perfect,* or completed perfectly his work on earth. In doing so he became the *source of eternal salvation.*

Reflection: *We are reminded that he is the "source of eternal salvation for all who obey him". This means making him Lord of our lives.*

A GREAT HIGH PRIEST

We have a great high priest who has gone through the heavens, Jesus the Son of God, (Hebrews 4:14).

IN THE BOOK OF Hebrews the Lord Jesus is referred to twenty-four times as either *a Priest* or *a High Priest* and once as a *great High Priest*. There are also three references to him in the New Testament as *a sacrifice of atonement* (Romans 3:25, 1 John 2:2; 4:10).

Here the language of the Old Testament is used to indicate that the death of Jesus achieved what the sacrifices of the Old Testament could never achieve—a once for all cleansing from sin for all who have faith in his atoning death (Romans 3:25).

Therefore, on the basis of his high priestly work for us, we now have *confidence* to enter the presence of God with hearts that are *sprinkled to cleanse us from a guilty conscience* (Hebrews10:19–22).

Reflection: *"Such a high priest meets our need" (Hebrews 7:26). Remember to thank the Lord Jesus for his work as your Great High Priest.*

A PRIEST FOREVER IN THE ORDER OF MELCHIZEDEK
(Hebrews 7:17, quoting Psalm 110:4)

MELCHIZEDEK IS FIRST MENTIONED in Genesis 14:18–20. His name means King of Righteousness and King of Salem (Jerusalem) or King of Peace. He was also the priest of God Most High, and blessed Abraham on his return from battle. There is no background history to Melchizedek, so the writer of Hebrews referred to him as a *priest forever* (Hebrews 7:3).

Aaron was a priest under the law of Moses and the representative of the old covenant which had become *weak and useless* (7:18). Being *in the order of Melchizedek* the Lord Jesus has a superior priesthood to that of Aaron (7:11), for the Lord Jesus became *the guarantee of a better covenant* (7:22).

The priests who followed Aaron all died, *but because Jesus lives forever, he has a permanent priesthood* (7:24).

Reflection: *Jesus as our high priest meets our need because he is able to save completely those who come to God through him, and because he intercedes for us (7:25).*

THE GUARANTEE OF A BETTER COVENANT
(Hebrews 7:22)

WHEN WE PURCHASE GOODS a written guarantee assures us of the quality of our purchase. So for Jesus to *become the guarantee of a better covenant* means that his life, death, resurrection, and ascension to heaven, provide us with a personal assurance that the *covenant* he established with God the Father is superior to the old covenant.

God's Old Testament covenant with Moses was based on the law and the people's obedience to this law. The law set the standard and made people conscious of their sins, but it had no power to help people live a holy life.

Christ's new covenant is *better*, because there is a better outcome. Righteousness is no longer achieved through obedience to the law but by faith in Christ. By trusting Christ for our salvation we are made righteous (Romans 5:19).

Reflection: *A question: Do we become right with God through our efforts to be good or by trusting in Christ as the guarantee of a better covenant?*

THE MEDIATOR OF THE NEW COVENANT
(Hebrews 9:15)

A MEDIATOR IS A person who is appointed for the purpose of dealing with the differences between people and of reconciling them to each other. During Abraham's lifetime God spoke directly to him, but when the law was given to Moses, it was the angels who took the role of mediator (Galatians 3:19).

The covenant statement outlined in the Ten Commandments (Exodus 20:3–17) set the standard of holiness, and the law outlined the sacrifices which were intended to restore men and women in their relationship with God.

For God to put in place a new and better covenant he needed a mediator who would be better than the angels. The only person who could fill this position was his own Son who, as *the mediator of the new covenant*, sealed the agreement between God and man with his own blood.

Reflection: *Because we have been reconciled to God by the work of "the Mediator", it follows that we should be reconciled to each other.*

A RANSOM
(Hebrews 9:15)

IN JEWISH CULTURE THE payment of a ransom was a common practice. Slaves could be redeemed by a close relative or "kinsman redeemer" (Leviticus 25:47–49), and there was the Jewish custom called "the Redemption of the Firstborn".

God had spared the lives of the firstborn sons of Israel on the night of the first Passover, (Numbers 3:13). In the years that followed, the firstborn sons were thought to belong to God and so had to be redeemed by the payment of five shekels to the priests (Numbers 18:16).

In Hebrews 9:15 the writer speaks about the death of the Lord Jesus as a ransom. The emphasis is on the price he paid by his death in order that sinners could be set free.

Reflection: *The death of Christ was a ransom for all men (1 Timothy 2:6), but the Gospels view his death as a ransom for many (Matthew 20:28; Mark 10:45). His ransom is therefore sufficient for the redemption of all, but effective for only those who believe.*

THE ARCHITECT AND BUILDER
(Hebrews 11:8–10)

The writer in the book of Hebrews makes the contrast between the temporary nature of Abraham's unsettled existence, with his vision of a permanent *city with foundations whose architect and builder is God.* The words for *architect* and *builder* indicate a skilled craftsman who can create the design and then build the structure.

Abraham was not promised a *permanent city* in his lifetime, so he endured the difficulties of a nomadic life while holding to the promise that he would be blessed through his descendants.

His vision of a *permanent city* is one that we have too. *We do not have an enduring city, but we are looking for the city that is to come* (Hebrews 13:14). It is nothing less than a home prepared for us by *the Architect and Builder.*

Reflection: *What a difference it makes to our lifestyle knowing that, like Abraham, we are pilgrims and strangers in this world and that the Architect and Builder has a place prepared for us.*

THE AUTHOR AND PERFECTER OF OUR FAITH
(Hebrews 12:2)

The writer of the book of Hebrews knew that to focus on the Lord as the *author and perfecter of our faith* meant having a right understanding of what the Lord Jesus has done for us.

The Lord Jesus "authored" our faith by coming to earth, making his Heavenly Father known to men and women and taking the punishment for our sin by dying for us.

As the "perfecter" or "finisher" *of our faith,* he perfectly completed this work of redemption and is now seated *at the right hand of the throne of God* (12:2) where he intercedes for us and is preparing a place for us. His position in glory indicates that God was completely satisfied with the work of his Son.

Reflection: *The theme of the book of Hebrews is the supremacy of the Lord Jesus. The writer knew that if his readers would fix their eyes on Jesus, then they would endure their troubles and stay true to him as his followers.*

THE JUDGE OF ALL MEN
Hebrews 12:23; James 5:8, 9

BOTH GOD THE FATHER and the Lord Jesus are spoken of by the title of *Judge*.

The Psalmist noted God's dual role of sovereign ruler and adjudicator when he said, *"The Lord reigns . . . He will judge the people with equity"* (Psalm 96:10).

However, in the New Testament we read that God has delegated this authority to his Son. *The Father judges no one, but has entrusted all judgment to the Son* (John 5:22).

Now a day of judgment is coming where we must all *give an account to him who is ready to judge the living and the dead* (1 Peter 4:5). Judgment for sinners will mean eternal separation from God (Matthew 13:49), but for God's people judgment will be an evaluation, where we will either gain or lose our reward (1 Corinthians 3:12–15).

Reflection: *Paul looked forward to the award of a "crown of righteousness" from the "righteous Judge" (2 Timothy 4:8). Knowing that we all face his judgment should affect the way we live.*

OUR GLORIOUS LORD JESUS CHRIST
(James 2:1)

JUST AS DAVID ACKNOWLEDGED God as the *God of glory* (Psalm 29:3), so *our glorious Lord Jesus Christ* is the risen Lord whom Christians own and worship. The *Spirit of glory* also shares this glory of God and we are reminded that *the Spirit of glory and of God rests on* us (1 Peter 4:14).

It is difficult for us to grasp how the magnificence of God's glory should be seen in us, but irrespective of our race or status in society, our salvation in Christ ensures his presence and his glory.

Therefore, as James said, we should not *show favoritism* to some Christians who are rich and then ignore or despise those who are poor. To act in this way is to demean the glory of the Lord that is to be seen in his people.

Reflection: *"Our glorious Lord Jesus Christ" will be seen in us as we demonstrate his love and live our lives to "the praise of his glory" (Ephesians 1:12).*

Names for, and References to, God the Son, our Lord Jesus Christ

THE GREAT SHEPHERD OF THE SHEEP
(Hebrews 13:20)

IN JOHN'S GOSPEL THE Lord Jesus is presented as the *good shepherd* (John 10:11), for he laid down his life for the sheep when he died on the cross to reconcile men and women to God.

As the *great Shepherd of the sheep*, God has raised him from death (Hebrews 13:20) and through him has equipped us *with everything good for doing his will* (13:21). The purpose of his work in us is that we might be *pleasing to him* (13:21), as we submit to his authority and obey him.

In the same way as a shepherd in Bible times led his sheep, so our *great Shepherd* has the ongoing task to *work in us* (13:21) encouraging, strengthening and leading us.

Reflection: *Pray that the great Shepherd of the Sheep may work in you, giving you everything you need for life and godliness through your knowledge of him (2 Peter 1:3). Thank him today for this great provision.*

THE NOBLE NAME
(James 2:7)

THIS DESCRIPTIVE TITLE, THE *noble name*, is a reference to Christ and appears in some Bible translations as a "worthy" or "honorable" name. James says that we belong to the "noble name", meaning that we belong to Christ.

The word is translated from the Greek word *kalos* meaning "good", but its meaning goes beyond the moral goodness of a person to referring to their actions as being pleasing and beautiful.

It is easy to see why James used the word *kalos* as a description for the name of Christ, for it associates the person of the Lord Jesus with the beauty of his character and behavior. For instance, he was the *good (kalos) Shepherd* (John 10:11).

Reflection: *Owning his name should mean that we worthily represent him as we seek by his grace to reflect his glory and grow in his likeness (2 Corinthians 3:18). Remember, it is the loveliness of a person's life that draws others to Christ as much as what we say and do.*

A LAMB WITHOUT BLEMISH

... You were redeemed ... with the precious blood of Christ, a lamb without blemish or defect (1 Peter 1:18, 19).

THE WORD REDEMPTION HAS the idea of a payment made in order to settle a debt, so for a slave to be set free, someone had to pay the redemption price to the owner of the slave.

In the New Testament the word redemption includes this idea of deliverance or ransom, and how that release was obtained through *the precious blood of Christ*. Peter reminded his readers that their redemption had been from bondage to an *empty way of life* passed down through their culture and that the redemption price was paid through Christ's blood.

In this verse the permanent and lasting nature of Christ's redemption is contrasted with the *perishable* or temporary nature of a monetary payment.

Reflection: *Peter states that our response to God's love in providing his Son as a "Lamb without blemish or defect", should be to "love one another deeply from the heart" (1 Peter 1:22).*

THE SHEPHERD AND OVERSEER

For you were like sheep going astray, but now you have returned to the Shepherd and Overseer of your souls, (1 Peter 2:25).

PETER'S USE OF THE title *the Shepherd* is a reference to the ongoing work of our Lord Jesus in caring for the sheep who *have returned to* him.

The expressions *going astray* and *returning* contrast our former position, of being spiritually lost and distant from *the Shepherd*, with our now secure position under the care and supervision of *the Shepherd*.

The reference to our Lord as the *Overseer* emphasizes his authority to direct the affairs of the Church and the lives of his followers. Those within the Church who have leadership responsibilities therefore need to be attentive to the direction the Lord brings through his Word.

Reflection: *The two titles of Shepherd and Overseer therefore bring together the ideas of the Lord as a loving Shepherd who feeds and cares for his people, and as an Overseer who guides us and directs the affairs of the Church.*

THE LIVING STONE
(1 Peter 2:4)

IN 1 PETER 2, the Lord Jesus is referred to as a *Living Stone* (2:4), *a precious Corner Stone* (2:6) and *a Capstone* (2:7). These metaphors of a "stone" present the Lord Jesus as an integral part in the building of his Church.

He is a *Living Stone*, for he gives life and indwells his Church by his Holy Spirit. As the *chosen and precious Corner Stone*, Jesus gives the orientation and design for the building (2:6). As the *Capstone*, his position in the Church is like a "head stone" or "head of the corner" on the top of the building that completes the structure (1 Peter 2:7).

The Lord Jesus therefore has the position of preeminence as Head of his Church.

Reflection: *Peter thus presents an image of the Lord Jesus as the foundation and the Head of the Church, and its source of life. For unbelievers however, Jesus warned that they would fall and be crushed by this stone (Luke 20:18).*

CHRIST AS LORD
But in your hearts set apart Christ as Lord, (1 Peter 3:15).

IT WAS THE PRACTICE in the Roman Empire prior to the crucifixion of a prisoner to require the condemned person to carry his cross through the city in front of the onlookers. The procession was a salutary reminder to the people that any crime would be harshly punished.

For the prisoner about to die, carrying the cross was a final symbolic statement that he was being forced to submit to the authority of Rome.

The disciples of Jesus would no doubt have been surprised when Jesus said to them: *If anyone would come after me, he must deny himself and take up his cross and follow me.* (Matt. 16:24)

Reflection: *Note the connection between what was said by Jesus and Peter. We take Peter's advice "to set apart Christ as Lord" when we obey the command of Jesus and submit to his authority taking up his cross and following him.*

THE CHIEF SHEPHERD

(1 Peter 5:4)

IT WAS THE USUAL practice for a shepherd in Bible times to bring his sheep home at the end of the day to the safety of the sheepfold. Peter draws on this imagery to refer to our Lord as the *Chief Shepherd* who will one day come for his "sheep" and bring them to the glory of his Father's presence.

The *crown of glory* is the reward awaiting his "sheep" that have followed him faithfully. This reward stands in contrast to the laurel wreath awarded to the winner at an ancient sporting event which will fade away.

The *crown of glory . . . will never fade*. Peter presented this metaphor of the *Chief Shepherd* in a context in which he also addressed the Church leaders as "shepherds". As "shepherds" serving the *Chief Shepherd* they were to be examples in serving the flock.

Reflection: *As the sheep of his pasture (Psalm 100:3); we should live our lives in expectation of his coming to take us to the safety of his home.*

OUR LORD AND SAVIOR

(2 Peter 3:2)

THE NAMES LORD AND *Savior* highlight two aspects of Jesus' ministry.

As *Savior*, Jesus was born to earth as the promised "Anointed One", or Christ/Messiah, who would be the *Savior* to redeem Israel. However, he was rejected by the Jewish people, so salvation was extended to those without a Jewish heritage. Among the first "outsiders" to acknowledge him was a group of Samaritans who said, *we know that this man really is the Savior of the world* (John 4:42).

The name "Lord" in the New Testament embraces ideas from the two Old Testament names for God: "YHWH" and "Adonai". YHWH or "LORD" (in capital letters), emphasizes his eternal self-existence and his covenant relationship with mankind. The name "Adonai", or "Lord" (in lower case letters), acknowledges his authority as Master. While many people knew him only as "Jesus of Nazareth", to his disciples he was always their *Lord* (John 21:12).

Reflection: *To know Jesus as our Savior means we must also know his authority in our lives as our Lord. As Peter said, he is "our Lord and Savior".*

NAMES FOR, AND REFERENCES TO, GOD THE SON, OUR LORD JESUS CHRIST

OUR LORD AND SAVIOR JESUS CHRIST
(2 Peter 3:18)

THIS BRACKET OF NAMES occurs three times in Peter's second letter. In chapter 1:5–8 Peter lists some qualities of Christian character and assures us the end result of a godly life will be *a rich welcome into the eternal kingdom of our Lord and Savior Jesus Christ* (1:11).

The second reference comes as a warning about false teachers and being entangled and overcome by evil (2:20). Peter says to *escape the corruption of the world* is to *know our Lord and Savior Jesus Christ* (2:20).

The third reference occurs when Peter encourages his readers *to grow in the grace and knowledge of our Lord and Savior Jesus Christ* (3:18). We *grow in grace* and in knowledge as we demonstrate the love of Christ to others and learn from him.

Reflection: *Note the link between the three mentions of his name: Growing in grace and knowledge of him will help guard against the corruption of this world and ensure a rich welcome into his eternal kingdom.*

THE LIFE, THE ETERNAL LIFE
(1 John 1:2)

IN BOTH HIS GOSPEL and in this letter John seeks to explain how Jesus is *the life*. The Gospel of John for instance records a series of vivid word pictures of Jesus as the "life".

He called himself *the bread of life* (6:35), *the resurrection and the life* (11:25) and *the way the truth and the life* (14:6), and spoke of people who followed him as having *the light of life* (8:12). John also stated that the purpose in writing his gospel was that people *by believing may have life in his name* (20:31).

Knowing that Jesus is the source of life and the giver of life means that there is an invitation for all to share in his *eternal life*.

Reflection: *Jesus Christ is the true God and eternal life (1 John 5:20). Did you realize that sharing eternal life with Christ means sharing the life of the true God, whose life has a divine quality and is everlasting?*

THE RIGHTEOUS ONE

We have one who speaks to the Father in our defense . . . Jesus Christ, the Righteous One, (1 John 2:1).

THE LORD JESUS SPEAKS to the Father in our defense because he is the *Righteous One*. We are told that *there is now no condemnation for those who are in Christ Jesus* (Romans 8:1) because the Father sees us as sharing in the righteousness of Christ. Paul explained how this happened when he said, *God made him who had no sin to be sin for us, so that in him we might become the righteousness of God* (2 Corinthians 5:21).

As the *Righteous One*, his Kingdom is established in the lives of his people and is characterized by *righteousness, peace and joy in the Holy Spirit* (Romans 14:17).

Therefore, righteous living should characterize our behavior for as members of his spiritual kingdom, we are *created to be like God in true righteousness and holiness* (Ephesians 4:24).

Reflection: *One day "the Righteous One" will be the "Righteous Judge" of all men.*

THE ADVOCATE

(1 John 2:1, KJV)

IN JOHN'S GOSPEL, THE Greek word *Parakletos* is a title for the Holy Spirit and is translated "Comforter" (KJV), and "Counselor" (NIV), (John 14:16). However, the word can also be translated "Advocate" and in this case refers to someone who stands alongside an accused person to defend them in court.

John takes this legal term and uses it in reference to the Lord Jesus. He says, *I write this to you so that you will not sin. But if anybody does sin, we have one (an Advocate) who speaks to the Father in our defense—Jesus Christ, the Righteous One* (1 John 2:1).

While Satan continues to accuse us day and night before the Father (Revelation 12:10), fortunately there is no case for us to answer for our *Advocate speaks to the Father in our defense.*

Reflection: *The charges against us are dismissed, not because of any merit in us, but entirely on the basis that "the blood of Jesus . . . purifies us from all sin"* (1 John 1:7).

THE ATONING SACRIFICE

He is the atoning Sacrifice for our sins, (1 John 2:2).

The offering of an *atoning sacrifice* was an Old Testament practice where the Israelite priests made sacrifices for the sins of the people. These sacrifices only "covered over" their sin, but the sin remained unpunished waiting the day when Christ would pay the penalty on the cross, (Romans 3:25).

The sacrifices renewed the people's relationship with a holy God and were thus released from the guilt of their sin. These sacrifices had to be repeated, because God's law acted as a standard for behavior but had no power to help people live a holy life.

To remedy this situation Christ, as our substitute, died as the *atoning sacrifice* and in dying he appeased or set aside God's wrath so that his sacrifice for us never had to be repeated, (Heb. 10:10).

Reflection: *Christ's atoning sacrifice brought cleansing from sin, so we can now "draw near to God, having our hearts sprinkled to cleanse us from a guilty conscience" (Hebrews 10:22).*

THE SAVIOR OF THE WORLD

(John 4:42)

It was the Samaritans who said, *we know that this man really is the Savior of the world*.

On some occasions this salvation was in the form of a healing, as when Jesus healed or saved (*sozo*) the woman who had been bleeding for twelve years (Matthew 9:20–22). Most often however, it was salvation from sin that is referred to.

There is also the sense that Jesus continues to deliver or save us on a daily basis, for as Paul says, *having been reconciled, shall we be saved through his life* (Romans 5:10). In this sense we have the experience of his on-going salvation.

But we also look forward to our future salvation when the Lord comes for his Church. Paul says, *our citizenship is in heaven. And we eagerly await a Savior from there, the Lord Jesus Christ* (Philippians 3:20).

Reflection: *Believers can say, we are saved, we are being saved and we shall be saved. Our salvation in Christ is a complete salvation.*

THE TRUE GOD

He is the true God and eternal life, (1 John 5:20).

OUR UNDERSTANDING OF TRUTH shapes not only our Christian faith but influences the way we act and react. Both God the Father and the Son are revealed by this title—*the true God* (Jeremiah 10:10; 1 John 5:20). As the *true God*, the Son is not only true to his word, but gives us an understanding of himself through his presence in our lives. *We are in him who is true* (1 John 5:20).

John now challenges his readers: *Dear children, keep yourselves from idols* (1 John 5:21). Idols are the false gods that we construct for ourselves and can be anything that takes the place of God in our lives.

The outcome of having false gods such as material possessions is that *the true God* ceases to be the person that makes life meaningful, for we find our meaning in substitute gods.

Reflection: *Who is it that we worship, "the true God" or the idols of our own making?*

JESUS CHRIST, THE FATHER'S SON

Grace, mercy and peace from God the Father and from Jesus Christ, the Father's Son, (2 John 1:3).

KNOWING THAT JESUS CHRIST is the Father's Son assures us of his divinity and so God's blessings of *grace, mercy and peace* are also blessings from his Son.

- *Grace* is the undeserved favor of God provided for us in Christ.
- *Mercy* flows from God's grace bringing help to those in need.
- *Peace* is the enjoyment of a restored relationship with *God*.

In any Church the basis of fellowship is the truth of God's word and his grace, mercy and peace shown in our love and service to others. John therefore gives the discussion a personal perspective by his own example in being able to *love in the truth* (1:1).

Reflection: *Knowing the God of truth (Psalm 31:5) through his revelation to us in Jesus Christ, the Father's Son, gives us a foundation to live in the truth and demonstrate his grace, mercy and peace to others.*

THE NAME

It was for the sake of the Name that they went out, (3 John 7).

A NAME IDENTIFIES A person and sometimes gives an indication of a person's character or reputation. When John wrote this title *"the Name"*, he knew his readers would understand the expression as personifying the Lord Jesus.

It was *in his Name* and *for the sake of the Name* that the Apostles went out to preach the gospel. These words indicate that what they did had the authority of the Lord Jesus and was done on his behalf. It was Jesus who said that *repentance and forgiveness of sins will be preached in his name* (Luke 24:47).

The outcome of this preaching resulted in people believing and being saved through *his name, for there is no other name under heaven given to men by which we must be saved* (Acts 4:12).

Reflection: *Remember when we pray in "his name", we are praying to the Father using the authority of the Lord Jesus to make our petition.*

HE WHO IS HOLY AND TRUE

To the angel of the church in Philadelphia write: These are the words of him who is holy and true, who holds the key of David, (Revelation 3:7).

THE TITLE HOLY AND *true* is ascribed to God in Revelation 6:10, but the title is also ascribed to Christ indicating the essential unity of the Father and the Son. As the One who *is holy and true*, the Lord Jesus addressed the Church, holding *the key of David* (Revelation 3:7).

This is a reference to King David giving Eliakim the honor of holding the key to the royal palace in Jerusalem with authority to open and close doors (Isaiah 22:20–24)

These words are now used of *"him who is holy and true"*, who has authority to open or close the door that admits or shuts people out of his kingdom.

Reflection: *It must have been an encouragement for these Christians to read this letter and to be assured of an open door into the kingdom of God (Revelation 3:8).*

THE AMEN, THE FAITHFUL AND TRUE WITNESS

To the angel of the church in Laodicea write: These are the words of the Amen, the faithful and true witness (Revelation 3:14).

THE WORD "AMEN" IS used at the end of a prayer with the meaning "so let it be," but the word is also a name of the Lord Jesus. John writes in the name of *the Amen*.

In the Old Testament *the Amen* was a name of God (Isaiah 65:16), but in the same way as *God, the Amen,* was truthful to his promises, so this name for Jesus emphasizes that, as the *Amen,* he is a *faithful and true witness*.

The Apostle John's message to the Church at Laodicea is a strong rebuke to this Church for its lukewarm attitudes, and so the name *Amen the Faithful and True Witness* gives emphasis that this message from the Lord is reliable.

Reflection: *For us to be truthful and reliable is to have the character of "the Amen, the faithful and true witness".*

OUR ONLY SOVEREIGN AND LORD

They are godless men, who change the grace of our God into a license for immorality and deny Jesus Christ our only Sovereign and Lord (Jude 4).

JUDE WROTE HIS LETTER to the Church to take a stand against the actions of *godless men*. The words *a license for immorality* indicate that they sanctioned immoral living as a lifestyle. But to call Jesus Christ the *only Sovereign and Lord* informs us that these *godless men* had no authority for their teaching.

Such immorality destroyed the connection between Christian belief and responsible Christian behavior, and set aside Christ's teaching about his people living holy lives.

The Greek word for *Sovereign* is "despotes" which means master, and the word *Lord* comes from the Old Testament names "Adonai" (Lord) and "YHWH" (LORD). As *our only Sovereign and Lord,* Jesus Christ therefore has absolute authority in his Church.

Reflection: *People still misrepresent God's grace when they deny the authority of the "only Sovereign and Lord". Make sure you have a belief that behaves.*

THE FIRSTBORN FROM THE DEAD

Jesus Christ, who is the faithful witness, the firstborn from the dead (Revelation 1:5).

THE SEVEN CHURCHES OF Asia were facing a time of trial and so John wanted them to be assured of God's wonderful provision for them. He explained that Jesus had lived his life on earth as a *faithful witness* demonstrating his Father's love and sharing the truth about himself with others.

The title of *firstborn* (Colossians 1:15), had indicated his unique position of honor as God's *one and only Son* (John 3:16), but the title, *the firstborn from the dead,* refers to his resurrection, (1 Peter 1:18, 19).

His resurrection complemented his work on the cross and was proof that he had conquered sin and death. To be the *firstborn from the dead* indicates that others will follow his resurrection, (Romans 6:5).

Reflection: *As "the firstborn", our Lord has all honor and power, but as "the firstborn from the dead", he gives us hope of an eternal future with him in the glory.*

I AM THE FIRST AND THE LAST . . . THE LIVING ONE

"Do not be afraid. I am the First and the Last. I am the Living One . . . And I hold the keys of death and Hades, (Revelation 1:17, 18).

IN REVELATION, JOHN WAS overwhelmed by this vision of the glorious risen Lord Jesus as he revealed himself as the *I Am, the First and the Last, the Living One.*

The "I Am" name is equivalent to the Old Testament name *YHWH,* or LORD, who is self-existent and always present. As the *First and the Last, the Living One,* he assured John of the eternity of his existence and that he is alive and active.

What a revelation it must have been for John now to see the Lord Jesus in his glory and with all authority holding *the keys of death and Hades, a* symbol of his authority to judge.

Reflection: *To understand the greatness and authority of our risen Lord by this name is to appreciate that life after death is in his control.*

THE RULER OF GOD'S CREATION
(Revelation 3:14)

As the *Ruler of God's creation* the Lord Jesus is its beginning cause, being first in time and first in his position of power and authority.

In this role he was assessing the Church at Laodicea which was on the trade route east of Ephesus. The people thought of themselves as being financially independent, blessed with the best eye medicines and clothed with the finest of garments. But these were symbols of their decline, for God saw them as *poor, blind and naked* (Revelation 3:17).

They had created a financially secure world for themselves, but were ignoring the *ruler of God's creation* who was the source of their existence and so he gives a warning that he was about to *spit* them out of his mouth (3:16).

Reflection: *Having wealth provides opportunities for Christians to be generous to others in need, but wealth becomes a curse when we allow it to rule our lives. Knowing "the Ruler of God's creation" should give us a proper perspective on life.*

THE LION OF THE TRIBE OF JUDAH
(Revelation 5:5)

Judah was an ancestor of King David and of the Lord Jesus (Matthew 1:3–16). On the occasion when Jacob blessed each of his sons it was Judah who was identified as a "lion's cub" (Genesis 49:9, 10). In later scriptures Judah is also pictured as a lion (Micah 5:8; Numbers 24:9).

In Old Testament times the lion was common in Palestine and Scripture alludes to its strength, courage and roar as symbols of its power and aggression. During the forty years that Israel spent in the desert after their release from slavery in Egypt, it was the tribe of Judah who led the other tribes in procession with their banner featuring a lion (10:14).

Reflection: *In heaven it is the Lord Jesus who is the Lion of the tribe of Judah. He is proclaimed to be worthy because of his triumph over Satan at the cross and his redemption of people from every tribe, language and nation, (Revelation 5:2–5).*

NAMES FOR, AND REFERENCES TO, GOD THE SON, OUR LORD JESUS CHRIST

THE WORD OF GOD

He is dressed in a robe dipped in blood, and his name is the Word of God (Revelation 19:13).

THE OCCASION IS THE *wedding supper of the Lamb* (19:7), and the church as the bride is dressed and ready to meet the Lord Jesus as the bridegroom. But when the bridegroom appears he is presented on a white horse leading the armies of heaven as the all-conquering *King of Kings and Lord of Lords* (19:16).

Both the bride (the Church) and the armies of heaven are dressed in *fine linen, bright (white) and clean* (19:8, 14). In contrast, the Lord Jesus is *dressed in a robe dipped in blood, and his name is the Word of God* (19:13).

For his garments to be dipped in blood symbolizes his on-going victory. This victory started at the cross, but will be completed when his enemies are defeated.

Reflection: *We now await the indescribable glory of heaven when the "Word of God", the bridegroom, will be victorious over all his enemies.*

KING OF KINGS AND LORD OF LORDS

(Revelation 19:16)

SATAN SAW THE DEATH of Jesus as a victory, but the crucifixion resulted in Satan's hold over creation being broken. Now in his vision John saw the Lord and he gives four names to the rider on a white horse who goes forth to conquer the nations (19:11–17).

- He is called *Faithful and True* (19:11).
- He has a name that is not revealed to us (19:12).
- He is the *Word of God* (19:13).
- He is *the KING of KINGS and LORD of LORDS* (19:16).

His victory is described as *treading the winepress of the fury of the wrath of God Almighty* (19:15). The imagery is of a trough of grapes being trampled and so his enemies will be crushed.

Reflection: *We either choose to accept Jesus as our Savior and Lord now or face his judgment in the future. It is then that everyone will acknowledge that he is "KING of KINGS and LORD of LORDS".*

A STAR, A SCEPTER
(Numbers 24:17)

ON THE OCCASION WHEN the Israelites crossed the plains of Moab on their way to the Promised Land, the King of Moab hired a diviner called Balaam to curse the Israelites so that they could be more easily defeated in battle.

Three times the king went with Balaam to places where he sacrificed to his gods in preparation for Balaam to make his curse. However, each time the Lord gave Balaam words of blessing for Israel.

The king was furious, but Balaam gave this wonderful prophecy about the future leader of Israel. *A star will come out of Jacob; a scepter will rise out of Israel* . . . one who will be *a ruler* (24:17-9). The prophecy was partially fulfilled in King David, but more completely in the coming of the Messiah.

Reflection: *In the same way as sailors have used the stars to guide their ships by night, so the Messiah would be a future ruler, a star and a scepter who would be a guiding light with kingly authority to rule.*

A HORN OF SALVATION
He has raised up a horn of Salvation for us in the house of his servant David (Luke 1:69).

ZECHARIAH WAS THE FATHER of John the Baptist and spoke the above words prophetically on the occasion of John's birth, (1:69).

Old Testament writers referred to the ram's horn as a symbol of strength, so when David acknowledged that God was the source of his strength he said, *he is my shield and the horn of my salvation, my stronghold,* (Psalm 18:2).

The ram's horn was also used as a container and filled with oil for the anointing of national leaders, (1 Samuel 16:13). As a wind instrument the horn was blown as a signal to rally the army to battle, (Hosea 5:8), and in worship the horn was used to praise the Lord, (Psalm 98:6).

Reflection: *Zechariah's message about the impending birth of the Messiah as a "horn of salvation" must have quickened the interest of those godly people who awaited his coming and assured them of the strength of his leadership.*

Names for, and References to, God the Son, our Lord Jesus Christ

JESUS
(Matthew 1:21)

The name *Jesus* is the English form of the Hebrew name Joshua and means "the Lord saves". The name was first revealed to Mary by an angel, and Luke records his birth as Mary's story and outlined her ancestral record (Luke 1:31). An angel also revealed the name *Jesus* separately to Joseph and it was his story and his family history that Matthew records (Matthew 1:16–25).

You can imagine how Joseph and Mary would have shared with each other their accounts of the angels' visits. Each of them had been given the name *Jesus*. Mary had the additional information about his reign on the throne of David with the names, the *Son of the Most High* and the *Son of God* (Luke 1:32, 35).

They also knew about the Old Testament "Immanuel" title—*God with us* (Matthew.1:23). With wonder and awe they would have cradled the new-born Jesus in their arms as they considered this amazing revelation.

Reflection: *We too continue to remember his birth and bow in worship before him.*

A CHILD, A SON
For to us a child is born, to us a son is given, (Isaiah 9:6).

A "child born" suggested that Immanuel's coming would be a normal childbirth, but a "son given" indicated the birth would be a special gift of God.

However, Isaiah's audience would not have appreciated that the son would be *the Son of God* (Matthew 14:33).

The frequent references to Jesus in his early years as *a child*, is the writer's way of indicating that there was nothing to indicate from his appearance that he was anything other than a normal boy. Since it was unlawful for parents to live in a place without a school we can assume he attended the local school at Nazareth, from the age of five or six years.

Reflection: *Luke beautifully reports, "Jesus grew in wisdom and stature and in favor with God and men," (2:52). Physically, mentally, socially and spiritually he developed his relationship with his heavenly Father as well as with the people of his community.*

THE ROOT OF JESSE

In that day the Root of Jesse will stand as a banner for the peoples,
(Isaiah 11:10).

The above title refers to a descendant of Jesse, King David's father, who would restore the fortunes of Israel.

In the time of Isaiah the glory of David's kingdom had long gone and the coming exile under the Assyrians and Babylonians had been foreshadowed (Isaiah 8:7, 8; 13:4, 5). Against this picture of despair the image of a *root* gives hope to the nation that it will "sprout" again with new life.

The reference here, and in the verses that follow, speak of both the return from exile in Babylon and of the Lord Jesus, who would become a *banner for the nations* (11:12). Paul affirms this event when he says, as the *Root of Jesse*, the Lord Jesus will *rule over the nations* (Romans 15:12).

Reflection: *At his first coming Jesus' right to rule was not recognized and he was crucified, but the day of judgment approaches when every knee shall bow and each will give an account of himself to God, (Romans 14:10-12).*

YOUR SALVATION, ... A LIGHT FOR REVELATION TO THE GENTILES, A GLORY TO YOUR PEOPLE ISRAEL

(Luke 2:30-32).

Mary and Joseph entered the Temple with the baby Jesus to offer a sacrifice and pay their five shekels as the "redemption price" for their firstborn son (Numbers 18:16). Simeon was there that day as a worshipper who had previously been told by the Holy Spirit that he would not die until he had seen the *Lord's Christ* (2:26).

Simeon immediately recognized the significance of the occasion when he held the baby Jesus and said: *"For my eyes have seen your salvation . . . a light for revelation to the Gentiles and for glory to your people Israel,"*

From their earlier encounters with the angel, Mary and Joseph knew something of who their baby would be (Matthew 1:20-22; Luke 1:26-33). Now their secret was known by someone else.

Reflection: *It was the scope of this salvation that must have surprised Mary and Joseph that day. No wonder Luke records that Joseph and Mary marveled at what was said about him (Luke 2:33).*

THE BRIGHT MORNING STAR

I am the Root and the Offspring of David, and the bright Morning Star (Revelation 22:16).

IN THE BIBLE, THE term "star" originally comes from a prophetic reference to a future national leader: *A star will come out of Jacob* (Numbers 24:17).

This prophecy was fulfilled in the person of King David, Israel's great leader, but the prophecy was also an early reference to the coming Messiah and was fulfilled when Jesus was born. Sadly the nation rejected him as their leader.

The reference by the Lord Jesus of himself as the *bright Morning Star* is recorded in the context of his promised return, *Behold I am coming soon* (Revelation 22:12). There is also his invitation to drink from him, (22:17), an invitation that remains open until he comes.

Reflection: *In the same way as the planet Venus is the morning star that heralds the dawning of a new day, so the bright "Morning Star" heralds the coming of Jesus and the dawning of a new age.*

I AM THE ALPHA AND OMEGA

I am the Alpha and Omega, the First and the Last, the Beginning and the End (Revelation 22:13).

ALPHA AND OMEGA ARE the first and last letters of the Greek alphabet and are taken as a title by the Lord God (Revelation 1:8), and the Lord Jesus (22:13). *First and last* and *beginning and end* are time markers, indicating Jesus *was with God in the beginning,* for it was *through him all things were made,* (John 1:2, 3).

As the *Omega*, we know that *the end will come, when he hands over the kingdom to God the Father after he has destroyed all dominion, authority and power,* (1 Corinthians 15:24, 25).

When the "I Am" name is included in the title, it becomes clear that the Lord Jesus is not just *the beginning and the end* of all things, but he is Sovereign Lord from beginning to end who *is Lord of all* (Acts 10:36).

Reflection: *What confidence we can have, that in a world of apparent uncertainty he is the "I Am, the Alpha and Omega".*

Names for, and References to, God the Holy Spirit

THE HOLY SPIRIT

Do you not know that your body is a temple of the Holy Spirit?
(1 Corinthians 6:19, 20).

THE *HOLY SPIRIT* IS the third person in the Godhead, so we worship One God but in three persons—Father, Son and Holy Spirit. The name *Holy Spirit* identifies him from the rest of the spirit world by the holiness of his being.

In Old Testament times the *Holy Spirit* anointed particular individuals for special tasks, (e.g. Exodus 35:30–32). Similarly, *men spoke from God as they were carried along by the Holy Spirit* (2 Peter 1:21). From the time of Pentecost (Acts 2:1–4), the Holy Spirit abides in every believer and is a "deposit", *guaranteeing our inheritance,* (Ephesians 1:14).

We also enjoy fellowship with him as we pray in the *Holy Spirit* (2 Corinthians 13:14; Jude 1:20). As our guide (John 14:26) he seeks to change us into the likeness of our Lord, (2 Corinthians 3:18), helping us to grow in holiness, (Romans 15:16).

Reflection: *What a life's partner we have to live with us!*

THE GIFT MY FATHER PROMISED

Do not leave Jerusalem, but wait for the gift my Father promised (Acts 1:4, 5).

AMONG THE LAST WORDS of Jesus before his ascension to heaven was this promise to his disciples of the gift of the Holy Spirit—*the gift my Father promised.*

Jesus had previously told the disciples about the coming of *another Counselor* who would *be with them forever* (John 14:16, 17); *and would guide them into all truth,* (16:13). During the next ten days they were *constantly in prayer* as they waited and no doubt thought about Jesus' promise.

The Pentecost event (Acts 2:1–4), changed everything for the disciples. Now with boldness Peter in his first message preached repentance and forgiveness of sins, baptism and the assurance that they would *receive the gift of the Holy Spirit* (Acts 2:38).

Reflection: *Gifts can be received with appreciation or they can be ignored and neglected. Allow the Holy Spirit—"the gift my Father promised"—to transform and empower you as he did the disciples.*

THE SPIRIT OF THE SOVEREIGN LORD

The Spirit of the Sovereign LORD is on me because the LORD has anointed me, (Isaiah 61:1).

THE TITLE "SOVEREIGN LORD" indicates that God has supreme authority, is eternal in his being and present in and beyond his creation. So for God the Holy Spirit to be given this title means that these attributes are also characteristic of his being.

Jesus applied this title from Isaiah to himself (Luke 4:18, 19) and thus indicated that he had the authority of *the Spirit of the Sovereign Lord* to carry out his ministry. Today the *Spirit* continues his ministry in the lives of believers.

Paul reminded us that our minds need to be controlled by the Spirit and that we should demonstrate this reality by being dead to sin and alive to righteousness (Romans 8:6, 10).

Reflection: *The "Spirit of the Sovereign LORD" gives you the spiritual authority and divine power to serve God in the same way that Jesus did. Think what this could mean for your life.*

MY SPIRIT

This is the word of the LORD to Zerubbabel: "Not by might nor by power, but by my Spirit", says the LORD Almighty (Zechariah 4:6).

WITH ZERUBBABEL AS GOVERNOR, the first group of Jewish captives to return to Jerusalem had the task of rebuilding the city and the temple. This rebuilding wasn't easy for the people surrounding Jerusalem sought to discourage and frighten them in their work, (Ezra 4).

However, Zechariah spoke the word of the Lord to reassure the people. The temple would be rebuilt, but it would not be accomplished *by might nor by power but by my Spirit*. The prophet Haggai also spoke encouragement from the Lord, *my Spirit remains among you. Do not fear* (Haggai 2:5).

For the Lord to refer to the Holy Spirit as *my Spirit* emphasizes his personal presence in working with and on behalf of his people.

Reflection: *In whatever way you serve the Lord remember it is "not by might nor by power, but by my Spirit" that his work will be accomplished.*

Names for, and References to, God the Holy Spirit

THE SPIRIT OF OUR GOD

But you were washed, you were sanctified, you were justified in the name of the Lord Jesus Christ and by the Spirit of our God (1 Corinthians 6:11).

PAUL SPEAKS OF OUR salvation as a process in which we are "washed, sanctified and justified". The symbol of washing indicates a cleansing from sin through the blood of the Lord Jesus.

Sanctification refers to the ongoing process of becoming like Christ in holiness. In being justified God declares us to be in a right relationship with himself through faith in the name of the Lord Jesus.

The *Spirit of our God* is also involved in this salvation process, for he firstly convicts us of our sin and our need to repent. Then as we turn to the Lord for cleansing so he brings us to spiritual birth in Christ (John 3:8).

Reflection: *The on-going work of "the Spirit of our God" needs our cooperation if he is to help us grow in our likeness to the Lord Jesus.*

THE HOLY SPIRIT SENT FROM HEAVEN

(They) . . . preached the gospel to you by the Holy Spirit sent from heaven (1 Peter 1:12).

IT IS THE *HOLY Spirit* who convicts of sin and brings a person to faith in Christ as their Lord and Savior, but it was the disciples who were given the great commission to "*Go and make disciples of all nations,*" (Matthew 28:19). This task is still ours today to be a witness to what God has done in our lives. As Peter said, we preach *the gospel . . . by the Holy Spirit sent from heaven.*

For people who have experienced salvation in Christ, there is an awareness of a spiritual transaction that makes them members of God's family. Paul explained this when he said, *The Spirit himself testifies with our spirit that we are God's children* (Romans 8:16).

Reflection: *Pray that the witness of your life and the words you speak will have the power of the "Holy Spirit sent from heaven" to bring the life of Christ into the lives of your friends.*

THE MIND OF THE LORD

Who has understood the mind of the LORD?—Spirit of the LORD—NIV alternative reading (Isaiah 40:13).

THE HEBREW WORD FOR "mind" in this verse is "ruah" and can be translated as "breath", "wind" or "spirit/Spirit". The *Mind of the Lord* can therefore be thought of as the *Spirit of the Lord*.

Isaiah considered the mind of the Lord as unfathomable in his knowledge and wisdom and beyond human comprehension. Therefore the question he asks is meant to encourage his people to trust the Lord, for he is *Sovereign* (40:10) and has no equal (40:25).

Paul quoted Isaiah 40:13 in 1 Corinthians 2:16, but the word that he used for *mind* was the Greek word "nous" that can mean "thinking", "understanding" or "insight. He asked *who has known the mind of the Lord?* This time he gives an answer, *we have the mind of Christ*.

Reflection: As believers we have God's Spirit as "the mind of the Lord". Therefore he has "lavished on us with all wisdom and understanding" (Ephesians 1:8).

STREAMS OF LIVING WATER

If anyone is thirsty let him come to me and drink. Whoever believes in me . . . streams of living water will flow from within him. By this he meant the Spirit (John 7:38, 39).

IN THE OLD TESTAMENT, water represented the spiritual refreshment available from God for people to drink from him (Isaiah 55:1). Water was also a symbol of the Holy Spirit who, like water poured out on a thirsty land, would one day be poured out on his people (Isaiah 44:3).

Ezekiel and Zechariah also saw Israel as a blessing to the nations as a river flowing out from the Temple (Ezekiel 47:1–12) and as living water flowing from Jerusalem (Zechariah 14:8).

In the New Testament Jesus explained that the person who received eternal life would have the presence of the Holy Spirit in his life as *streams of living water flowing from within him.*

Reflection: As individuals and as a Church, the life of Christ is meant to flow by his Spirit as a blessing to others who are thirsting.

HIS SPIRIT

But Moses replied, "Are you jealous for my sake? I wish that all the LORD'S people were prophets and that the LORD would put his Spirit on them" (Numbers 11:29).

MOSES WAS THE ANOINTED leader of Israel and he sensed that people were envious of him as they saw the power of God at work in his life.

Moses wanted God's best for Israel and it was his wish that all the *LORD'S people* should also enjoy the anointing of God's Spirit. However, in Old Testament times only God's chosen leaders had this anointing. This unfulfilled wish by Moses that *his Spirit* would come on all the people was eventually fulfilled on the day of Pentecost.

The people of Israel were the *Lord's people* by birth, but from the time of Pentecost, people from other nations also became the *Lord's people*. This is because they had their spiritual birth in Christ and had *his Spirit* within them.

Reflection: *Spiritual leadership is not driven by human wisdom but is under the direction of "his Spirit".*

THE BREATH OF THE ALMIGHTY

The breath of the Almighty gives me life, (Job 33:4).

IN THE ABOVE VERSE a person called Elihu affirmed that it was the *Spirit of God* who was God's agent in creation, and as the *breath of the Almighty* gave him his life.

The *Almighty* is a name for God that emphasizes his omnipotence. Elihu therefore knew that the Spirit worked with God's almighty power to give life and understanding to people, (Job 32:8). The *breath of the Almighty* continues to be the source of spiritual life and understanding for God's people.

The Hebrew and Greek words for "breath" also mean "wind" and it was Jesus who explained to Nicodemus that the blowing of the wind is like the coming of the Spirit to give people their spiritual birth (John 3:8).

Reflection: *The Holy Spirit, the "breath of the Almighty" will complete his work when he breathes life into our dead bodies on the day of our resurrection (Romans 8:11). What a future we have to look forward to.*

YOUR GOOD SPIRIT

Teach me to do your will, for you are my God; may your good Spirit lead me on level ground, (Psalm 143:10).

PSALM 143 RECORDS AN occasion when David's leadership was threatened and in the psalm he prayed for help while affirming the *faithfulness and righteousness of* the Lord (143:1).

David had experienced the Lord's goodness on many occasions so he was confident in making his request to the Lord. He wanted to be taught by the Lord and be led by his *good Spirit* on *level ground*.

All of us would like to live our lives on a "level playing field" where things go smoothly. But the "terrain" through which the Lord takes us is often difficult and like David we can become dismayed (143:4) or feel the Lord is not listening (143:7).

Reflection: *The terrain ahead may not be a level playing field. Disappointments and difficulties make life tough, but the Lord assures us that he will teach and guide us by his "good Spirit" as he did for David.*

A SPIRIT OF JUDGMENT

He will cleanse the bloodstains from Jerusalem by the Spirit of judgment (Isaiah 4:4).

IN ISAIAH 4:2–6 THERE is a prophecy about the Messiah. His coming was to be for the glory of Israel and through the *Spirit of judgment and the Spirit of fire* he would cleanse the nation. Israel needed to learn that *the LORD is with you when you are with him. If you seek him, he will be found by you* (2 Chronicles 15:2).

When Jesus was with his disciples he referred to the Spirit when he said, *when he comes, he will convict the world of guilt in regard to sin and righteousness and judgment* (John 16:8). The word "convict" means to "convince" as well as "to expose", and so in judging or evaluating our lives the *Spirit of judgment* alerts us to our need of repentance.

Reflection: *John said, if we confess our sins, he is faithful and just and will forgive us our sins and purify us from all unrighteousness (1 John 1:9).*

THE SPIRIT OF FIRE

He will cleanse the bloodstains from Jerusalem by the Spirit of judgment and the Spirit of fire, (Isaiah 4:4).

FIRE IS ASSOCIATED WITH God's judgment, for *God is a consuming fire* (Hebrews 12:29). But in the same way as metals are refined by fire, so fire is a symbol of God's purifying work.

It was this cleansing fire that God intended for Israel. God is a God of love, but he is also a holy God. Therefore, Israel needed the *Spirit of fire* to cleanse away the *bloodstains* of their sins.

John the Baptist announced the coming of Jesus with the words, *He will baptize you with the Holy Spirit and with fire* (Matthew 3:11). This prophecy was fulfilled at Pentecost, (Acts 2:3, 4). So with the Holy Spirit within us, Paul warns, *Do not put out the Spirit's fire,* (1 Thessalonians 5:19). We do this when we sin.

Reflection: *Allow the "Spirit of fire" to burn up the dross that hinders his work in your life.*

THE SPIRIT OF WISDOM AND UNDERSTANDING

(Isaiah 11:2)

ISAIAH FORETOLD THAT THE Spirit of the Lord would be seen in the life of the Messiah as *wisdom and understanding.*

As a Jew, Jesus lived in a society that was dominated by the Romans but also influenced by Greek thinking that viewed wisdom as the clever arguments of philosophers. Jesus, however, epitomized the Hebrew view of wisdom that focused on a godly lifestyle in which a person exercised sound judgment in the daily decisions of life.

As God's Son, Jesus lived his life with a perfect understanding of his Father's will that found expression in what he said and did as he ministered to the needs of others. Paul spoke of the Lord Jesus as the *wisdom of God* (1 Corinthians 1:24).

Reflection: *Just as the Holy Spirit was the Spirit of wisdom and understanding to Jesus, so he is to God's people today, for he gives understanding of God and spiritual wisdom to guide us in the decisions of life.*

THE SPIRIT OF COUNSEL AND POWER

The Spirit of the Lord will rest on him—the Spirit of counsel and power, (Isaiah 11:2).

THE HEBREW WORD FOR counsel means both "advice" and "plan", so for Messiah to live with the *Spirit of counsel* resting on him meant that the advice he gave to people was within the Spirit's plan for them.

But good counsel needs to be coupled with God's power if it is to change people's lives. His power was most evident in Jesus' miracles and healings.

Jesus also referred to the Holy Spirit as the *Counselor* (John 14:26), who would bring power to the lives of his followers, (Acts 1:8). So he is the *Spirit of counsel and power* for all believers today.

Reflection: *As the "Spirit of counsel and power" prompts your conscience and speaks to you through God's Word; his counsel is always within the context of his plan for you, and comes with his power to help you achieve God's will for your life.*

THE SPIRIT OF KNOWLEDGE AND THE FEAR OF THE LORD

The Spirit of the LORD will rest on him . . . the Spirit of knowledge and the fear of the LORD, (Isaiah 11:2).

THIS PROPHECY BY ISAIAH about the coming of the Holy Spirit to the Messiah was fulfilled publicly on the occasion when John the Baptist baptized Jesus (Matthew 3:16).

For us today, it is the *Spirit of knowledge* who brings spiritual understanding and insight from the Word of God. Through his abiding presence in our lives he convicts of sin, helping us to maintain our relationship with the Father.

Knowledge can also refer to the organization of experience, so again the *Spirit of knowledge* helps us to learn spiritual lessons from the experiences of life. While "fear" can be a negative emotion, for Christians, the "fear of the Lord" refers to an attitude of reverence and awe.

Reflection: *The Spirit's presence should release us from slavish conformity to the ways of the world, so that being released from fear we will have a love for God in which we worship and serve him.*

THE BREATH OF THE LORD

For he will come like a pent-up flood that the breath of the LORD drives along,
(Isaiah 59:19, 20).

Isaiah chapter 59 presents a bleak picture of Israel's sinfulness. However, the prophet looked forward to a brighter future when people would confess their sins committed against each other and acknowledge their rebellion and treachery against the Lord. (59:12–15).

The prophet knew that there was still hope of deliverance. He saw the Lord looking on and being *appalled that there was no one to intervene* (59:16).

But Isaiah also knew that *the arm of the Lord is not too short to save* (59:1). The Lord is presented in this passage as a warrior putting on his armor, (59:17), and ready to strike a blow at the enemy. It is the Holy Spirit, as *the breath of the Lord*, who drives the enemy away.

Reflection: *God is still at work and the "breath of the LORD" still accomplishes his purposes in a sinful world.*

POWER FROM ON HIGH

(Luke 24:49)

Prior to Jesus' return to heaven he assured the disciples of his Father's great promise, that they would be *clothed with power from on high*. This promise had been prophesized by Joel and referred to the coming of the Holy Spirit, (Joel 2:28).

The power of the Holy Spirit helps us in several ways. Firstly, he gives us victory over temptation, (1 Corinthians 10:13). Then through prayer, the Holy Spirit helps us in our battle against the powers of darkness. Paul says, *we have divine power to demolish strongholds.* (2 Corinthians 10:4).

The *power from on high* is evident in the gifts he gives to serve and bless others (Hebrews 2:4), while the fruit of the Spirit develops our character changing us into the likeness of Christ, (Galatians 5:22).

Reflection: *The Holy Spirit is the "power from on high" who brings his divine energy to help us live our lives in his strength. To be "filled with the Spirit" is to be filled with "power from on high".*

THE COUNSELOR

I will ask the Father and he will give you another Counselor to be with you forever, (John 14:16).

JESUS EXPLAINED TO HIS disciples that he was going back to his Father, and promised them that he would ask the Father to give them *another Counselor*. The Greek word for *Counselor* means a helper who comes alongside to strengthen and encourage. The word indicates that the *Counselor* would be another person of the same kind as Jesus.

Therefore, in the same way that the Lord Jesus had revealed the Father and strengthened and encouraged the disciples, so the *Counselor* would work with them.

But some things were going to be different. Jesus was about to leave them, so the disciples could now be assured that *the Counselor* would *be with them forever*.

Reflection: *Coping with the difficulties of life is not always easy, but it is the work of "the Counselor" to help us and enable us to live in the resurrection power of our Lord.*

A SPIRIT OF GRACE AND SUPPLICATION

And I will pour out on the house of David . . . a spirit of grace and supplication, (Zechariah 12:10).

TODAY ISRAEL AS A nation does not recognize Jesus Christ as the Savior of the world, but God has not forgotten his covenant with Israel, that *I will be your God and you will be my people* (Jeremiah 7:23). For this covenant promise to be fulfilled the nation must return in repentance and acknowledge Jesus Christ as their Lord. This will happen when the Holy Spirit is *poured out on the house of David,* (Israel).

As *the Spirit of grace* he will bring the favor of God to Israel ministering God's grace to believers as his children (Romans 9:26). As the *Spirit of supplication* his work is one of intercession in which he pleads to God for mercy on behalf of his people (Romans 8:27).

Reflection: *One day Israel will experience what Christians today have already experienced, the blessing of the Spirit of grace and supplication poured out on them.*

THE SAME GIFT

Then I remembered what the Lord had said . . . God gave them the same gift as he gave us, (Acts 11:16, 17).

PETER WAS CRITICIZED BY the Jewish Christians at Jerusalem because he had entered the house of non-Jewish people and had eaten with them (11:2, 3). Peter defended himself by explaining his vision and then the sequence of events that happened in Cornelius' house.

He reminded them of what Jesus had said about the baptism of the Spirit (11:16), and then convinced them by explaining that the *same gift* had now been given to these new non-Jewish believers.

What happened that day was a turning point in the life of the Jerusalem Church. Up until this time the Church regarded themselves as a group within Judaism. Now they realized the Church embraced non-Jewish people as well.

Reflection: *It is easy to think of the Jewish Christians at Jerusalem as prejudiced, but we too can be like that. Remember that all true believers share in "the same gift"—the Holy Spirit.*

THE SPIRIT OF JESUS

(Acts 16:7)

THE HOLY SPIRIT IS called the *Spirit of Jesus* because he was sent by the Father in the name of Jesus (John 14:26).

During Paul's second missionary journey, while traveling with Silas and Timothy, they were not sure in which direction to proceed. They were *kept by the Holy Spirit from preaching the word in the province of Asia* (Acts 16:6); and the *Spirit of Jesus* would not allow them to enter Bithynia (16:7).

They continued west and one night as they rested at Troas Paul was given a vision of a man from Macedonia (northern Greece) calling, *Come over to Macedonia and help us* (16:9). Now they knew where to go.

Reflection: *Knowing God's direction for our lives often has an element of uncertainty. However, the Christian experience is a life of faith in which we pray that the Lord will guide us and then we proceed, trusting the Spirit of Jesus to open or close doors and keep us going in the right direction.*

THE SPIRIT OF HOLINESS

His Son ... who through the Spirit of holiness was declared with power to be the Son of God by his resurrection from the dead: Jesus Christ our Lord, (Romans 1:3, 4).

THIS IS THE ONLY verse in which the Holy Spirit is referred to as *the Spirit of holiness*. It is the holiness of his character that arrests our attention when we hear this verse read.

But as the verse indicates, the *Spirit of holiness* is the Spirit of power, for it was at the resurrection of Jesus that his power was demonstrated and the identity of the *Son of God* authenticated.

It follows that Jesus Christ is Lord of all.

Reflection: *Before the coming of the Spirit, the Temple was the place of worship where God met with his people. Now the "Spirit of holiness" lives within us as his Temple, so worship of God requires us to live holy lives. We demonstrate this holiness by being separated to God from evil and being like Christ in the way we behave.*

THE SPIRIT OF LIFE

(Romans 8:2)

IN ROMANS 8:2, THE *law of the Spirit of life* is contrasted with *the law of sin and death*.

The Holy Spirit as the *Spirit of life* operates on the principle of bringing life and freedom into people's lives while the application of the law of Moses invariably results in sin and death. It is the *Spirit of life* who has set us free from sin and spiritual death.

The Old Testament law had the purpose of revealing the character of God to Israel. It showed that God was holy, and to be God's holy people they needed to adopt the standards outlined in the law. But by the law all men failed to achieve God's righteous standards.

Reflection: *The law of Moses had no power to change people's lives and men and women had no power to be holy. Now "the Spirit of life" has made the life of Christ in us a reality, giving us the power to live a holy life—Hallelujah.*

Names for, and References to, God the Holy Spirit

THE SPIRIT OF GOD

You, however, are controlled not by the sinful nature but by the Spirit, if the Spirit of God lives in you, (Romans 8:9).

IN THIS VERSE THE NIV translation uses the word "controlled" whereas the Greek clause could be translated, " *not in the flesh but in the Spirit*". But the meaning is clear; for the *Spirit of God* to be "in" our lives implies that he should be in control.

We trust in the Lord Jesus for our salvation but we must also acknowledge his authority over our lives by our obedience to the Scriptures, and by our submission to the control of the *Spirit of God*.

It is the *Spirit of God* who interprets Scripture to us by leading and guiding us *into all truth* (John 16:13).

Reflection: *Paul gives us the following definition of a Christian, "those who are led by the Spirit of God are sons of God" (Romans 8:14). Therefore, obedience to his leading and acceptance of his control in our lives is the ongoing test which indicates if we are truly his disciples.*

THE SPIRIT OF CHRIST

And if anyone does not have the Spirit of Christ, he does not belong to Christ, (Romans 8:9).

IN THE ABOVE VERSE Paul gives the defining characteristic of a Christian. They have the *Spirit of Christ* living within them.

The Holy Spirit is called the *Spirit of Christ*, for the Spirit was present and guided Jesus in what he did. For instance, we read that *Jesus, full of the Holy Spirit, returned from the Jordan and was led by the Spirit in the desert* (Luke 4:1).

But the Holy Spirit is also called the *Spirit of Christ* for Jesus sent him to us as our Counsellor and Guide, (John 16:7).

In the same way that the love of Jesus was seen when he healed the sick, so his love and concern for his disciples was seen when he sent his Spirit to them.

Reflection: *The "Spirit of Christ" continues to make Christ real to us today as he directs us to serve God through his empowering presence in our lives.*

THE SPIRIT OF HIM WHO RAISED JESUS FROM THE DEAD
(Romans 8:11)

PENTECOST SAW THE FULFILLMENT of Joel's prophecy about the coming of the Holy Spirit, (Joel 2:28). The Christians knew a new age had arrived and that the Holy Spirit would now be with them forever, just as Jesus had promised, (John 14:16).

The life of the Spirit in us sustains our spiritual union with Christ and assures us of the future resurrection of our bodies. The fact that the Spirit *raised Jesus from the dead* means that he will also give us new life (Romans 8:11).

At present we are mortal and death awaits us, but the wonderful truth is that there is the certainty of a resurrection to look forward to.

Reflection: *The future coming of Christ for his Church and the resurrection of our bodies is the living hope that Christians look forward to (1 Peter 1:3). What a difference this should make, because "everyone who has this hope in him purifies himself, just as he is pure" (1 John 3:3).*

THE SPIRIT OF SONSHIP
You received the Spirit of Sonship, and by him we cry, "Abba, Father" (Romans 8:15).

THE HOLY SPIRIT IS identified as *the Spirit of Sonship,* because of his work in testifying to our adoption as Sons, (8:16). Thus we are within a family relationship with God our *Abba* or Daddy/Father.

Five times in his writing, Paul used this image of adoption to draw attention to God's choice of us (Romans 8:15; 8:23; 9:4; Galatians 4:5; and Ephesians 1:5 KJV). The background of this expression comes from the Roman legal system where a father might adopt a son in order to preserve the family name.

The father had control over the life of his adopted child, while the child enjoyed all family privileges and was expected to bring honor to his new father.

Reflection: *The parallel that Paul made with the Roman adoption system highlights that we have a heavenly Father and that Satan no longer has any rights over us. We are now new persons with a new identity.*

THE SPIRIT

The Spirit helps us in our weakness. We do not know what we ought to pray for, but the Spirit himself intercedes for us with groans that words cannot express, (Romans 8:26, 27).

WE ARE NOT LIKELY to imagine Paul having a problem in praying. Yet his weakness like ours is identified as a failure to know how to pray. We usually think that *the Spirit's work* in us is to strengthen and guide us, but he also lives to *intercede for us with groans that words cannot express.*

To petition someone is to intercede and to groan is to express an intensity of feeling. So the petition of *the Spirit* to God the Father expresses the intensity of his concern for us.

Being God *the Spirit*, he knows perfectly what the Father's will is for us and so he is able to *intercede according to God's will.*

Reflection: *Have you ever thought of prayer as your area of weakness and that the Spirit intercedes for you perfectly according to the will of God?*

THE FIRST FRUITS OF THE SPIRIT

We ourselves, who have the first fruits of the Spirit, groan inwardly as we wait eagerly for our adoption as sons, the redemption of our bodies. For in this hope we were saved, (Romans 8:23, 24).

THE "FEAST OF FIRST fruits" (Leviticus 23:9–14), was a Jewish harvest festival celebrating the beginning of the harvest season.

The *first fruits of the Spirit* therefore indicates that we have received only a foretaste of the Holy Spirit, who will one day do a much greater and more complete work in us than we have experienced to this present time.

Like the Jewish farmers who looked forward to the main harvest, so Christians "groan inwardly" in eager expectation of what awaits them in the resurrection.

Reflection: *Is your groaning the grumble of dissatisfaction or the inner longing of your heart to be with your Lord in the glory? It will only be the latter if you appreciate the presence of the Holy Spirit in your life as "the first fruits" of a better life to come.*

THE SPIRIT WHO IS FROM GOD

We have not received the spirit of the world but the Spirit who is from God, that we may understand what God has freely given us, (1 Corinthians 2:12).

IN THIS VERSE PAUL makes the point that the *spirit of the world*, which refers to human wisdom, will never lead to knowledge of God. It is only the *Spirit who is from God* who can give us this spiritual understanding about God and all that he has given us.

This will include at least the following that he has given us:

- *a new birth into a living hope* (1 Peter 1:3).
- *the Spirit as a deposit, guaranteeing what is to come* (2 Corinthians 5:5).
- *different gifts, according to the grace given us* (Romans 12:6).
- *everything we need for life and godliness* (2 Peter 1:3).
- *his very great and precious promises* (2 Peter 1:4).

Reflection: *Pray that the "Spirit who is from God" will continue to help you understand what God has given you.*

THE HOLY SPIRIT WHO IS IN YOU

Your body is a temple of the Holy Spirit, who is in you,
(1 Corinthians 6:19, 20).

MANY IN THE CITY of Corinth lived an immoral lifestyle. For instance, there was the temple of Aphrodite, the goddess of love, where temple prostitution was elevated as a form of worship.

In contrast, Paul reminds the Corinthians that for holiness you must *honor God with your body* because you are the *temple of the Holy Spirit who is in you*. Knowing that our bodies are a spiritual temple should make us careful not to do anything that would defile our bodies and thus hinder our worship of the Lord.

Paul listed the sins of the flesh as *sexual immorality, impurity and debauchery; idolatry and witchcraft; hatred, discord, jealousy, fits of rage, selfish ambition, dissensions, factions and envy; drunkenness, orgies, and the like,* (Galatians 5:19–21).

Reflection: *What sort of a residence do you provide for the "Holy Spirit who is in you"? Remember to honor God with your body.*

Names for, and References to, God the Holy Spirit

THE ONE AND THE SAME SPIRIT

All these (spiritual gifts) are the work of one and the same Spirit, and he gives them to each one, just as he determines, (1 Corinthians 12:11).

THE PRESENCE OF THE Holy Spirit in our lives brings a range of gifting that enables us to contribute to the life of the Church.

Just as there is a variety of fruit (Galatians 5:22, 23), so there is a range of gifts. These gifts are enumerated for us in Romans 12:6–8; Ephesians 4:8–13 and in 1 Corinthians 12:7-11, and 27–31.

The exercise of gifts in the Corinthian Church caused jealousy and quarreling (3:3). Paul's answer was for the gifts to operate like the functioning of a human body, and thus enhance the work of the Church (12:12–30).

Reflection: *The fruit of the Spirit in our lives without the gifts of the Spirit means good character, but limited ability or power to accomplish the Lord's purposes. To have the gifts with no fruit means misguided ability and power that will do harm in the life of the Church.*

THE ONE SPIRIT

For we were all baptized by one Spirit into one body, whether Jews or Greeks, slave or free—and we were all given the one Spirit to drink, (1 Corinthians 12:12, 13).

ALTHOUGH THERE IS A great variety of people in the Church there is an essential unity in the body with Christ as the head (Ephesians 4:15).This unity should be seen in the functioning of the Church resulting from the presence of the *one Spirit* in the lives of God's people.

The statement that *we were all baptized by one Spirit into one body* refers to a spiritual baptism into Christ when we were given our spiritual birth in him as our Savior and Lord.

Twice in the book of Acts the coming of the Holy Spirit is said to have been *poured out* (Acts 2:33; 10:45) and so appropriately we were *given the one Spirit to drink.*

Reflection: *Remember, the presence of the "One Spirit" should help us preserve the unity of the Church, (Ephesians 4:3).*

THE SPIRIT OF THE LORD

Where the Spirit of the Lord is, there is freedom,
(2 Corinthians 3:17).

OF THE TWENTY-FOUR REFERENCES to the *Spirit of the Lord,* all but four occur in the Old Testament. Most of these references focus on the coming of the *Spirit of the Lord* to an individual to anoint them with power for some special purpose.

In the case of Gideon he belonged to an insignificant clan and was the least important member of his family (Judges 6:15). Yet, when the *Spirit of the Lord* came upon him (6:34), he was able to deliver his people from the Midianites.

It was the *Spirit of the Lord* who transformed David the shepherd boy into a great leader of the nation. From the day Samuel anointed him, *the Spirit of the LORD came upon David in power* (1 Samuel 16:13), to deliver the nation from their enemies.

Reflection: *Since Pentecost all Christians enjoy the presence of the "Spirit of the Lord" to empower them and free them from Satan's bondage.*

THE SPIRIT OF THE LIVING GOD

You show that you are a letter from Christ, the result of our ministry, written not with ink but with the Spirit of the living God, not on tablets of stone but on tablets of human hearts, (2 Corinthians 3:3).

PAUL HAD NO NEED to carry a letter of introduction as he had previously visited Corinth and was known to them. Paul therefore regarded these Christians as his *letter* or evidence as to the quality of his ministry.

At this time, the inks used in writing could fade or be wiped off the parchment. In contrast, *the Spirit of the living God* had written the message of life on the tablets of their hearts as a permanent message.

Paul notes that God's people are like letters *known and read by everybody.* Therefore *show that you are a letter from Christ* (2 Cor. 3:2, 3).

Reflection: *The people you work with can "read" you as they would read a letter. Make sure that they are reading "a letter from Christ".*

THE LORD WHO IS THE SPIRIT

And we, who with unveiled faces all reflect the Lord's glory, are being transformed into his likeness with ever-increasing glory, which comes from the Lord, who is the Spirit, (2 Corinthians 3:18).

PAUL REMINDED THE CORINTHIANS to reflect the Lord's glory for as they did this they would be *transformed* into the likeness of Christ. The word "transform" comes from the same Greek word as the word "metamorphosis" and both words refer to a striking change in appearance.

The caterpillar and the butterfly share the same genes, but the metamorphosis or transformation from a caterpillar to a cocoon and then to a butterfly results in a vastly different looking creature.

Reflection: *It is the "Lord who is the Spirit" who brings about this change in our lives. The end result will be our complete transformation into the likeness of the Lord Jesus, for as John said, "When he appears, we shall be like him, for we shall see him as he is" (1 John 3:2).*

THE SPIRIT OF HIS SON

Because you are sons, God sent the Spirit of his Son into our hearts, the Spirit who calls out "Abba Father" (Galatians 4:6).

IN GREEK CULTURE A boy was under the care of a trusted servant until the time of his initiation. This tutor had to ensure his moral development and good behavior and the boy had to obey his tutor in the same way any slave had to obey his master.

In Galatians 4:1–7 Paul likened the role of the tutor to the way the Old Testament law controlled people's lives (4:3).

So the law was put in charge to lead us to Christ (3:24). Now that faith has come we are no longer under the supervision of the law (3:25).

Reflection: *With the full rights of sons (4:5) we "have come of age". We are free from the old tutor, the law, and with the Spirit of his Son in our hearts he prompts us to thank and praise Abba Father for our freedom in Christ.*

THE PROMISE OF HIS SPIRIT

He redeemed us in order that the blessing given to Abraham might come to the Gentiles through Christ Jesus, so that by faith we might receive the promise of the Spirit, (Galatians 3:14).

GOD HAD CALLED ABRAHAM to leave his homeland for somewhere unknown and in response he trusted God and *obeyed and went, not knowing where he was going,* (Hebrews 11:8).

Abraham's obedience led to the blessing of a living relationship with God which has now come to all people who have faith in Christ's death for their salvation, (1 Peter 1:9).

We have also received the *promise of the Spirit,* which remained only a promise prior to the Spirit's coming, (Acts 2:4). Now the *promise of his Spirit* is a promise fulfilled for all believers who have faith in Jesus Christ.

Reflection: *The problem for many people is that they seek to achieve righteousness by their own efforts, but Paul restates the principle of Habakkuk 2:4, "the righteous will live by faith" (Galatians 3:11).*

A SEAL

Having believed, you were marked in him with a seal, the promised Holy Spirit, (Ephesians 1:13).

IN PAUL'S TIME THE sender of goods would place hot wax on a package at the point where it was fastened and the owner's stamp was pressed into the wax. This "mark" on the goods indicated the owner/sender and assured a person that the goods had not been opened.

When Paul used this image of a *seal* to refer to the Holy Spirit, he indicated that the Holy Spirit in our lives is God's *mark* of ownership upon us and that he will keep us secure until we go to be with him in the glory.

As Paul said to Timothy, *Nevertheless, God's solid foundation stands firm, sealed with this inscription: "The Lord knows those who are his".* (2 Timothy 2:19).

Reflection: *To be "marked in him with a seal" means that "nothing in all creation will be able to separate us from the love of God that is in Christ Jesus our Lord" (Romans 8:39).*

A DEPOSIT

Having believed, you were marked in him with a seal, the promised Holy Spirit, who is a deposit guaranteeing our inheritance until the redemption of those who are God's possession to the praise of his glory, (Ephesians 1:13, 14).

MAKING A DEPOSIT ON the purchase of some article is a common business practice. The deposit acts as an assurance that the buyer will make the full payment and thus complete the purchase.

For Paul to liken the Holy Spirit to a *deposit,* means that God is giving us a *guarantee* that the initial purchase of his people, through Christ's death for us, will be completed with the *redemption of those who are God's possession.*

The certainty of this coming event is, as Paul says, *to the praise of his glory.*

Reflection: *The word for an engagement ring in modern Greek comes from this word for a deposit. The deposit of the Holy Spirit is like the promise that comes with an engagement ring of a future union with the one we love.*

THE SPIRIT OF WISDOM AND REVELATION

I keep asking that the God of our Lord Jesus Christ, the glorious Father, may give you the Spirit of wisdom and revelation, so that you may know him better, (Ephesians 1:17).

EPHESUS WAS A CITY that prided itself in its worship of the Roman goddess Diana. Her temple was one of the seven wonders of the ancient world. Within this context Paul knew that the Christians needed the Holy Spirit to be with them as the *Spirit of wisdom and revelation.*

The Christians needed their knowledge of God to be coupled with good judgment as they expressed themselves and interacted in the community. Thus they needed spiritual wisdom.

But they also needed spiritual insight to interpret God's word and his will within the context of their Ephesian culture. Thus they needed to know their Lord better.

Reflection: *We too live in a heathen society and need to know our Lord better. Ask "the Spirit of wisdom and revelation" to share his wisdom and revelation with you.*

HIS POWER THAT IS AT WORK WITHIN US

Now to him who is able to do immeasurably more than all we ask or imagine, according to his power that is at work within us, (Ephesians 3:19, 20).

EARLIER IN THIS PRAYER Paul asked that the Ephesians might be *strengthened with power through his Spirit in your inner being* (3:16). The Greeks would have understood the "inner being" to be their minds and in particular their reasoning ability and their conscience.

The word for "power," refers to the authority and ability of the Holy Spirit to work in a way that we cannot measure or even imagine. Therefore, like the Ephesians, we should expect the Holy Spirit to be the *power that is at work within us,* who assists us in our thinking and helps us win the battle for the control of our minds.

Reflection: *Pray that the Lord will stretch your imagination so that you can appreciate more of what his power can achieve in and through you.*

THE HOLY SPIRIT OF GOD

And do not grieve the Holy Spirit of God, with whom you were sealed for the day of redemption (Ephesians 4:30).

IN THE SAME WAY that people can be offended by others, so the *Holy Spirit of God* can be grieved by our bad attitudes or behavior. Examples that Paul gives include, *unwholesome talk* and a failure to build others up *according to their needs* (Ephesians 4:29). In chapter 4:31 he lists other offensive behaviors. Thus we grieve the Holy Spirit when we hinder or silence him from speaking to us and working in our lives.

John the Baptist used "fire" as a symbol of the Holy Spirit's presence, (Matthew 3:11).

As fire, the Spirit *burns up the "chaff" in our lives* (Matthew 3:12), for he is concerned for our holiness and wants to get rid of anything that would hinder our spiritual development in becoming like our Lord. Therefore it is God's holy people whom he seals ready for the day of our redemption.

Reflection: *Guard your life and the life of your Church so that nothing is done that will "put out the Spirit's fire" and grieve the "Holy Spirit of God".*

Names for, and References to, God the Holy Spirit

THE SPIRIT OF JESUS CHRIST

I will continue to rejoice, for I know that through your prayers and the help given by the Spirit of Jesus Christ, what has happened to me will turn out for my deliverance, (Philippians 1:18b, 19).

FOR PAUL, DELIVERANCE COULD mean his release from imprisonment which he confidently expected (1:19). But it could also mean the possibility of his execution (1:20–23), in which case he would be free to be with his Lord.

Paul therefore contrasted his past experience of *what has happened* (1:19), with the uncertain future of *whatever happens* (1:27).

Knowing the help of the *Spirit of Jesus Christ* he could advise the Philippians, *Whatever happens, conduct yourselves in a manner worthy of the gospel of Christ . . . stand firm in one spirit, contending as one man for the faith of the gospel* (1:27).

Reflection: *Our Christian experience of "what has happened" should give us the confidence to believe that "whatever happens" in the future, the "Spirit of Jesus Christ" will be with us to guide and sustain us.*

HIS HOLY SPIRIT

For God did not call us to be impure, but to live a holy life. Therefore, he who rejects this instruction does not reject man but God, who gives you his Holy Spirit, (1 Thessalonians 4:7–8).

AGAINST THE BACKGROUND OF an immoral society at Thessalonica, Paul took an uncompromising stand for sexual purity and marital faithfulness (4:1–8). Not to accept this teaching was to reject *God who gives you His Holy Spirit.*

Further, to know that God is holy and that his *eyes are too pure to look on evil* (Habakkuk 1:13), is to appreciate why we need to keep ourselves pure, for our bodies are *the temple of the Holy Spirit,* (1 Corinthians 6:19).

Paul now explained that the presence of *his Holy Spirit* in our lives will result in relationships which demonstrate a genuine form of *brotherly love* (1 Thessalonians 4:9).

Reflection: *With the help of his Holy Spirit, "Put on the new self, created to be like God in true righteousness and holiness" (Ephesians 4:24).*

THE HOLY SPIRIT WHOM HE POURED OUT

He saved us through the washing of rebirth and renewal by the Holy Spirit, whom he poured out on us generously through Jesus Christ our Savior, (Titus 3:6).

THE SPIRIT WAS FIRST poured out on the Jews at Pentecost (Acts 2:33) and on the first Gentile Christians in the house of Cornelius (Acts 10:45). In this letter to Titus, Paul uses three words to beautifully summarize and explain the salvation process—*washing*, *rebirth* and *renewal*.

Washing refers to the cleansing of our sins through the blood of Christ (Ephesians 2:13).

Rebirth is figurative language for our entry into our life in Christ (John 3:3).

Renewal refers to the transforming work of the Holy Spirit as he changes us into the likeness of Christ (2 Corinthians 3:18).

Reflection: *Salvation then is both a completed work and a work in progress. Washing and rebirth gets us started in the Christian life, while renewal by the Holy Spirit empowers us and keeps us going, (Ephesians 5:18).*

SPIRIT OF TRUTH

(John 14:17)

THE TITLE, THE SPIRIT of Truth, is mentioned three times in John's gospel. In John 14:16, 17 Jesus says, *And I will ask the Father, and he will give you another Counselor to be with you forever—the Spirit of truth*. So it is the Counselor, the Spirit of Truth who brings God's abiding presence to our lives.

Secondly, in (15:26), the Counselor is again identified as the Spirit of Truth whose work it is to testify on behalf of the Lord Jesus. He does this as he draws people to faith in Christ.

Thirdly, Jesus told his disciples that, *when he the Spirit of truth comes, he will guide you into all truth*, (16:13).

So it is the work of the Spirit to give God's people an understanding of the truth concerning the Lord Jesus.

Reflection: *The "Spirit of Truth" abides in you as your Counselor to lead you into all truth. Pray that you will become more sensitive to his presence in your life.*

Names for, and References to, God the Holy Spirit

THE ETERNAL SPIRIT
(Hebrews 9:14)

ABRAHAM REFERRED TO GOD as the "Eternal God" (Genesis 21:33), and the Apostle John referred to Jesus as *the true God and eternal life* (1 John 5:20). It is not surprising therefore that the Holy Spirit, as the third person in the Godhead, is called *the eternal Spirit*.

Hebrews 9:14 explains that it was through *the eternal Spirit*, that Jesus *offered himself unblemished to God* as the perfect sacrifice for our sins.

Jesus lived his life on earth, not as God but as man, depending on the presence and power of the *eternal Spirit* to sustain and enable him. In this way Jesus modeled for us how life on earth should be lived in the power of the Spirit.

Reflection: *From the book of Hebrews we see what Jesus did for us has an eternal quality. He obtained for us eternal redemption, (9:12), through becoming the source of eternal salvation (5:9) and establishing an eternal covenant, (13:20), so that we may receive an eternal inheritance (9:15).*

THE SPIRIT OF GRACE

How much more severely do you think a man deserves to be punished who has trampled the Son of God under foot and who has insulted the Spirit of grace?
(Hebrews 10:29)

THE WRITER USED THE strongest of language to describe the rejection of Jesus and his offer of salvation. To "trample on the Son of God" and to "treat his blood as unholy" is to despise what Jesus has done for us.

Since it is the work of the Holy Spirit to convict people of their sin (John 16:8), this rejection of salvation in Christ is also an insult to the *Spirit of grace*.

The Holy Spirit is called the *Spirit of grace* because he administers God's grace, bringing about our spiritual birth and making us *sons of the living God* (Romans 9:26).

Reflection: *God continues to demonstrate his grace by doing special things in the lives of people through the "Spirit of grace". We must be careful to "listen" to what the Spirit is saying to us.*

THE SPIRIT HE CAUSED TO LIVE IN US

Or do you think Scripture says without reason that the Spirit he caused to live in us longs jealously?
(James 4:5—NIV alternate reading)

JAMES WROTE THESE WORDS to a group of Jewish Christians whom he accused of being an "adulterous people" (4:4). The picture is of people that had forgotten their covenant relationship and were unfaithful to their Lord.

James therefore reminded them (4:5) about the *jealous longing* or intense envy that the Spirit feels about their relationship with their Lord. In the verses that follow, James reminded the Christians of God's grace and his readiness to forgive and to restore them in their relationship with himself.

Thirteen times in the Old Testament, God is described as being a jealous God and so *the Spirit he caused to live within us* is also grieved when we sin, (Ephesians 4:30).

Reflection: *Remember that the Spirit has a jealous longing for you as he yearns for you to live a holy life (1 Peter 1:15-16).*

THE SPIRIT OF GLORY

For the Spirit of glory and of God rests on you (1 Peter 4:14).

THE HOLY SPIRIT HAS the name *the Spirit of glory*, for by his presence in our lives he represents to us both *the God of glory* (Psalm 29:3) *and the Lord Jesus, who is the* Lord of glory (1 Corinthians 2:8). The *Spirit of glory* brings to the lives of Christians the character of Christ so that his holiness and love form part of our new nature.

Peter explained that God's people can expect to be persecuted (4:12–19), but should learn to rejoice and endure while continuing to *do good* (v19).

In the Gospels, God's glory was evident in the person and work of the Lord Jesus, but now in the age of the Church, the *Spirit of glory and of God rests on you.*

Reflection: *"And we, who with unveiled faces all reflect the Lord's glory, are being transformed into his likeness with ever-increasing glory, which comes from the Lord, who is the Spirit" (2 Corinthians 3:18).*

Names for, and References to, God the Holy Spirit

THE POWER OF THE MOST HIGH

The angel answered, "The Holy Spirit will come upon you, and the power of the Most High will overshadow you. So the holy one to be born will be called the Son of God" (Luke 1:35).

What a shock it must have been for Mary to be told by the angel Gabriel that she will give birth to a son called Jesus. The angel also said that *he will be great and will be called the Son of the Most High* and that he will *reign over the house of David* (1:32, 33).

To be the *Son of the Most High* would mean that her boy would be the *Son of God*.

To *reign over the house of David* indicates that he would be the long awaited Messiah, (Isaiah 11:1–5).

Reflection: *Mary conceived by "the power of the Most High" and thus Jesus was truly God, but being born of Mary he was truly man. We too are born of human parents but are given spiritual birth by the "power of the Most High".*

THE SPIRIT HE GAVE US

And this is how we know that he lives in us: We know it by the Spirit he gave us, (1 John 3:24).

The Apostle John wrote about the deception that people experience when they fail to live by the truth of God's Word. Four times he accused such people of lying: (1:6; 2:4; 2:22; 4:20). These are strong words to use, but this truth needs to be emphasized because their behavior and beliefs affected their relationship with God, and their attitudes affected their relationships with other people.

John summarized this teaching in 1 John 3:24, about *believing* and *obeying* when he said, as Christians we *believe in the name of his Son,* and we obey when we *love one another.*

To *believe in his name* is to trust the Lord as our Savior. To love one another means to act towards others in the manner that Jesus demonstrated throughout his life.

Reflection: *When we believe and obey, John says we live in him and he lives in us.*

THE SEVENFOLD SPIRIT

Grace and peace to you from him who is, and who was, and who is to come, and from the sevenfold Spirit before his throne, and from Jesus Christ, who is the faithful witness. (Revelation 1:4, 5—NIV alternative reading)

THE NUMBER SEVEN INDICATES perfection and so the *sevenfold Spirit* is available in his completeness to the seven Churches to whom John was writing. The *sevenfold Spirit* is also *before the throne*, which means he is in the presence of God.

Here God the Father is named as *him who is, and who was, and who is to come,* with Jesus named as *the faithful witness.*

The Godhead was therefore giving a blessing of *grace and peace* to the seven churches in Asia. Five of the Churches are called to repent, but to all seven there was a promise to those who overcame.

Reflection: *We too have been given "very great and precious promises" (2 Peter 1:4), but remember the promises of the "sevenfold Spirit" are to those who overcome.*

Index of Names for, and References to, God the Father

Abba Father, 50
Ancient of Days, The, 43
Arm of the Lord, The, 40
Blessed and Only Ruler, The, 67
Compassionate and Gracious God, The, 11
Consuming Fire, A, 59
Dew of Israel, The, 68
Eternal King, The, 39
Everlasting and Eternal God, The, 6
Faithful Creator, A, 62
Father of Compassion, The, 53
Father of Heavenly Lights, The, 60
Father of spirits, The, 59
Father of the fatherless, a Defender of widows, 26
Forgiving God, A, 29
Glorious Crown, a Spirit of Justice, a Source of Strength, A, 34
Glorious Father, The, 55
Glory of Israel, The, 15
God, Creator of Heaven and Earth, 3
God Almighty, 6
God and Savior of Israel, The, 35
God Most High, 4
God of all Comfort, The, 53
God of all Grace, The, 62
God of all the Earth, The, 37
God of Bethel, The, 7
God of Glory, 22
GOD of Gods and LORD of Lords, 13
God of Heaven, 17
God of Hope, The, 52
God of Jeshurun, 12
God of Love, The, 54
God of Peace, The, 56
God of the Jews, the God of the Gentiles, 51
God of Truth, The, 24
God Our Father, 54

God Over All, 17
God the God of Israel, 7
God who knows, A, 15
God who Saves Me, The, 27
God who sees me, The, 5
God, the Blessed and Only Ruler, 57
Great and Awesome God, The, 18
Great God, The, 3
He who is and who was and who is to come, 64
Him Who is Able, 55
Holy One of Israel, The, 35
Holy One, The, 30
Hope of Israel, The, 40
I Am the Alpha and Omega the Almighty, 65
Immanuel, 32
Immortal God, The, 51
Judge, The, 50
King Eternal, Immortal, Invisible, the Only God, The, 56
King of all the Earth, The, 25
King of Glory, The, 21
King of Heaven, The, 42
King of kings and Lord of lords, 58
King of the Ages/Nations, 64
Light of Israel . . . the Holy One a Flame, 32
Living Father, The, 49
Living God, The, 38
Lord Almighty, The, 14
Lord God Almighty, The, 66
LORD God, The, 4
Lord is my Banner, The, 9
Lord is My Helper, The, 60
Lord is Peace, The, 14
Lord is There, The, 42
LORD is your Shade, The, 30
Lord of all the Earth, The, 13
LORD of Hosts, The, 67

Index of Names for, and References to, God the Father

Lord of the Harvest, The, 49
LORD Our God, The, 46
Lord our Maker, The, 28
Lord our Righteousness, The, 41
LORD Strong and Mighty, the LORD Mighty in Battle, The, 23
LORD, the God of the Hebrews, The, 66
Lord the God of Israel, The, 39
LORD the LORD, 33
Lord who heals you, The, 8
Lord who makes you Holy, The, 12
Lord whose name is Jealous, The, 10
Lord will provide, The, 9
LORD your God, The, 45
Lord your Maker, The, 36
Majestic Glory, The, 63
Majesty in Heaven, The, 58
Maker of Heaven and Earth, The, 29
Merciful God, A, 11
Mighty God, The, 33
Mighty One of Israel, The, 31
Mighty One of Jacob, The, 8
Mighty One, The, 65
My Father, 48
My God the Rock, 28
My Hiding Place, 25
My Husband, 44
My King and My God, 19
My Lamp, 16
My Light, My Salvation, My Stronghold, 23
My Presence, 10
My Rock, My Fortress, My Deliverer, 20
My Shepherd, 22
My Shield and the Horn of My Salvation, 21
My Strength, My Fortress, My Loving God, 26
My Stronghold, My Refuge, My Savior, 16
O LORD our Lord, 19
One Enthroned in the Heaven, The, 18
One I Praise, The, 41
One Lawgiver and Judge, The, 61
One Who Breaks Open the Way, The, 46
One Who is able to Save and Destroy, The, 61
Only God Our Savior, The, 63
Only Wise God, The, 52
Potter, The, 37
Praise of Israel, The, 20
Pride of Jacob, The, 45
Prince of Princes, The, 43
Redeemer, Our, 36
Refiner and Purifier, A, 48
Refuge, A, 47
Rock of Israel, The, 34
Ruler of All Things, 24
Savior of All Men, The, 57
Shepherd of Israel, 27
Sovereign Lord, The, 5
Spring of Living Water, The, 38
Strong Tower, A, 31
Wall of Fire, A, 47
Watchman over Ephraim, The, 44

Index of Names for, and References to, God the Son

Advocate, The, 134
Alpha and Omega, I Am the, 145
Amen, The Faithful and True Witness, The, 138
Anointed One, The, 103
Apostle and High Priest, The, 123
Architect and Builder, The, 127
Atoning Sacrifice, The, 135
Author and Perfecter of our Faith, The, 127
Author of Life, The, 102
Author of their Salvation, The, 80
Beginning, The First-born from the dead, The, 116
Branch, The, 74
Bread of God, The, 83
Bread of Life, The, 91
Bridegroom, The, 96
Bright Morning Star, The, 145
Carpenter The, Mary's Son, 115
Chief Shepherd, The, 132
Child, A Son, A, 143
Chosen One, The, 74
Christ as Lord, 131
Christ Jesus our Hope, 119
Christ of God, The, 96
Christ our Passover Lamb, 108
Christ the Power of God, 107
Christ the Son of the Living God, 99
Christ the Wisdom of God, 107
Christ who is God over all, 104
Christ, The (Messiah), 73
Consolation of Israel, The, 73
Covenant for the People, A, 84
Deliverer, A, 105
Everlasting Father, 79
Exact Representation of His Being, The, 122
Firstborn from the dead, The, 139
First Fruits, The, 110
Fragrant Offering and Sacrifice, A, 115

Friend of Taxpayers and Sinners, The, 97
Gate of the Sheep, The, 92
God, The One and Only, 81
Good Shepherd, The, 92
Great High Priest, A, 124
Great Shepherd of the Sheep, The, 129
Guarantee of a Better Covenant, A, 125
He Who Had No Sin, 75
He who is Holy and True, 137
Head over every Power and Authority, The, 117
Head that is Christ, The, 114
Heir of all Things, The, 121
Holy and Righteous One, The, 102
Holy One of God. The, 90
Hope of Glory, The, 117
Horn of Salvation, A, 142
Husband, A, 112
I Am the First and the Last, the Living One, 139
I, I Am, 90
Image of the Invisible God, The, 116
Indescribable Gift, His, 112
Jesus, 143
Jesus Christ is Lord, 111
Jesus Christ the Father's Son, 136
Jesus Christ the Son of God, 75
Jesus is Lord, 104
Jesus of Nazareth, 100
Judge of all Men, The, 128
KING OF Kings and LORD OF Lords, 141
King of the Jews, The, 97
Lamb of God, The, 86
Lamb without blemish or defect, A, 130
Last Adam, The, 110
Life, The, The Eternal Life, 133
Light for the Gentiles, A, 85
Light of the World, The, 91
Lion of the Tribe of Judah, The, 140

Index of Names for, and References to, God the Son

Living Bread, The, 88
Living Stone, The, 131
Lord, The, 93
Lord and Christ, 101
Lord of Peace, The, 119
Lord Jesus Christ, Our, 118
Lord of All, The, 105
Lord of both the dead and the living, 106
Lord of Glory, The, 109
Lord of the Sabbath, 89
Man accredited by God, A, 100
Man Christ Jesus, The, 120
Man from Heaven, The, 111
Man He has Appointed, The, 103
Man of Sorrows, A, 98
Man, A, 88
Master in Heaven, A, 118
Master, The, 120
Mediator of the New Covenant, The, 126
Messenger of the Covenant, 81
Mighty God, The, 78
My Lord and my God, 95
Name, The, 137
Noble Name, The, 129
One Greater than Jonah/Solomon, The, 95
One He Loves, The, 113
One who makes men holy, The, 123
One who was going to Redeem Israel, The, 98
Our Glorious Lord Jesus Christ, 128
Our great God and Savior Jesus Christ, 121
Our Lord and Savior, 132
Our Lord and Savior Jesus Christ, 133
Our only Sovereign and Lord, 138
Our Peace, 114
Our Righteousness, Holiness and Redemption, 108
Physician, The, 99
Priest forever in the order of Melchizedek, A, 125
Prince and Savior, A, 101

Prince of Peace, 80
Prophet, A, 87
Rabbi, 89
Radiance of God's Glory, The, 122
Ransom, A, 126
Resurrection and the Life, The, 93
Righteous One, The, 134
Righteous Servant, My, 72
Rising Sun, The, 85
Rock, The, 109
Root of Jesse, The, 144
Ruler of God's Creation, The, 140
Ruler who will be a Shepherd, A, 87
Savior of the World, The, 135
Servant of the Jews, A, 106
Servant, My, 71
Shepherd and Overseer, The, 130
Shiloh, 83
Shoot, A, 71
Son of David, The, 76
Son of God, The, 77
Son of Man, The, 77
Son of the Blessed One, 78
Son of the Most High, 72
Son, The, 76
Source of Eternal Salvation, The, 124
Star, a Scepter, A, 142
True God, The, 136
True Light, The, 86
Way the Truth and the Life, The, 94
Witness to the People, a Leader, A, 84
Wonderful Counsellor, 79
Word of Life, 82
Word, The, 82
Word of God, The, 141
Your Lord and Teacher, 94
Your Salvation—A Light of Revelation, 144
Your Seed, 113

Index of Names for, and References to, God the Holy Spirit

Breath of the Almighty, The, 153
Breath of the Lord, The, 157
Counselor, The, 158
Deposit, A, 169
Eternal Spirit, The, 173
First fruits of the Spirit, The, 163
Gift My Father Promised, The, 149
His Holy Spirit, 171
His Spirit, 153
Holy Spirit of God, The, 170
Holy Spirit sent from Heaven, The, 151
Holy Spirit whom He poured out, The, 172
Holy Spirit, The, 149
Holy Spirit who is in you, The, 164
Lord who is the Spirit, The, 167
Mind of the Lord, The, 152
My Spirit, 150
One and the Same Spirit, The, 165
One Spirit, The, 165
Power from on High, The, 157
Power of the Most High, The, 175
Power that is at work within us, His, 170
Promise of His Spirit, The, 168
Same Gift, The, 159
Seal, A, 168
Sevenfold Spirit, The, 176
Spirit He caused to live in us, The, 174
Spirit He gave us, The, 175
Spirit of Christ, The, 161

Spirit of Counsel and Power, The, 156
Spirit of Fire, The, 155
Spirit of Glory, The, 174
Spirit of God, The, 161
Spirit of Grace and Supplication, The, 158
Spirit of Grace, The, 173
Spirit of Him who raised Jesus from the dead, The, 162
Spirit of His Son, The, 167
Spirit of Holiness, The, 160
Spirit of Jesus Christ, The, 171
Spirit of Jesus, The, 159
Spirit of Judgement, A, 154
Spirit of Knowledge and the Fear of the Lord, The, 156
Spirit of Life, The, 160
Spirit of Our God, The, 151
Spirit of Sonship, The, 162
Spirit of the Living God, The, 166
Spirit of the Lord, The, 166
Spirit of the Sovereign Lord, 150
Spirit of Truth, The, 172
Spirit of Wisdom and Revelation, The, 169
Spirit of Wisdom and Understanding, The, 155
Spirit who is from God, The, 164
Spirit, The, 163
Streams of Living Water, 152
Your Good Spirit, 154

www.ingramcontent.com/pod-product-compliance
Lightning Source LLC
Chambersburg PA
CBHW080401170426
43193CB00016B/2784